R U N N I N G

Y O U R

O F F I C E

Margaret Korving

BBC Books

This book accompanies the BBC Radio series *Running your office*, first broadcast on Radio 4 VHF/FM from April 1988. The series was devised by Graham Tayar in association with the Royal Society of Arts (RSA) Examinations Board and the Open College.

Published by BBC Books, a division of

BBC Enterprises Ltd,
Woodlands,
80 Wood Lane,
LONDON W12 0TT

First published 1989

ISBN 0 563 34350 8

Photoset in 10/12 Ehrhardt and printed and bound in Great Britain by
Redwood Burn Limited, Trowbridge, Wiltshire

Cover printed by Fletchers of Norwich

Acknowledgements
Cover illustration by Ainslie MacLeod and illustrations on pages 11, 24, 29, 45, 62, 77, 83, 99 and 115. Artwork on pages 14 and 72 by Richard Geiger.

Contents

Foreword

Some people choose to run an office, others find they are promoted into running an office, and there are others who have running an office forced upon them.

If you are setting up a small business, you will certainly need an office where people can contact you and where you can keep records of orders, costs and information. If you are already working in an office, you may have your eye on a more interesting job with better pay and more responsibility once you have gained skills in office organisation.

You may be in your first job after leaving college, or a woman returner, nervous about dealing with new technology introduced since you last went to work. You could also be what is called a 'second jobber', i.e. someone who has coped pretty well in a first, junior job, and now looks for something better. *Running your office* is meant to help all of you.

In the sections that follow, you will find out how to manage your own job; meet office deadlines; develop telephone skills; deal with people (pleasant and unpleasant!); use communication systems (from letters to fax); manage manual and computer files; tackle research and report on it; arrange and minute meetings and develop your personal skills so you can carry on regardless of heavy workloads, difficult colleagues or time pressures.

Sounds a tall order? Not when you know how – and you soon will.

1 'What do you think you're doing?'

- What's your job really about?
- Will you be happy in a small office, a large office or the branch office of a big company?
- Are you on the look-out for ways to please your colleagues and make progress in your job?

Tell someone you are an accountant, and they will see a ledger. Say you are a doctor, and they can visualise the stethoscope round your neck. If you work in an office, your background is a desk, a phone and filing cabinet. Every job has an image, sometimes a rather out-of-date one: most offices nowadays have a computer.

But no two offices are the same. Shy young people will often say 'I'd like to work in an office', thinking that they will be behind the scenes, dealing with papers and files. Well, it might be like that some of the time. But sooner or later telephones start ringing, people begin asking questions, and you discover that there are meetings to attend and new technology systems to learn. Being 'behind the scenes' certainly does not mean being out of the action.

Small can be busy

Woman returning to work after a break may say, 'I think I'd like to begin with a job in a small office – just until I get used to things, you know.' They may just find such a haven in a quiet professional office where nothing much has changed in the last ten years. They might equally well end up working for a solicitor who has computerised all the records, or with someone just starting in business who expects their right-hand-person to be able to cope with everything from invoices to courier services.

Office workers are unique in being able to pick just about any environment they want to work in. There really are as many different kinds of offices as there are kinds of activity. You can work in a hospital office, a publishing office, an architect's office, a theatrical agent's office. There are farm and estate offices, social service offices, sales promotion offices, school and college offices, opera company offices. Whether you want to work for a Member of Parliament, a TV current affairs team, a fashion designer or a charity for the homeless, there will be an office job on offer sooner or later.

The more skills you gain in your first job, the more jobs you may be able to pick and choose from later (or you may become so capable that you are promoted before you have a chance to look for anything new!).

But just as no two office jobs are alike, so each individual office job has its own special demands. This chapter is headed 'What do you think you're doing?' because quite often it is up to the office employee to find that out.

Self-starters

When companies say that they want 'initiative', what they often mean is that they want someone who will look around and find out what is not being done, and get on with it. Or someone who will find a better, quicker way of coping with routine; or who will make use of quiet moments in the day or week to learn extra skills (which might be anything from using the telex to dealing with the office printing system).

To decide which skills will be most useful, first of all you need to know what your main job responsibilities might be. They may have been set out in writing in your contract of employment or explained in a conversation. What they involve in practice will depend on the kind of service the office provides, and for whom.

Who does the office serve?

It may be a *Head Office*, a *specialised department* or a *branch office*. They each provide services for groups of users.

A small firm with just a few employees needs an office as a central point for communication. It is where clients can get in touch; where the sales people can call in with orders; and where the taxman and VAT inspector can send their forms. It is the place where records are kept, messages taken, correspondence sent out and received, and meetings held. If you work in this sort of office, one of the first things to do is to find out who does what (*see page 9*) so that you can sort out enquiries,

6

letters and callers, and direct them to the right person. You will also have to find out where you fit in so that you can liaise with these people (*see page 12*).

With a large firm, there is also likely to be a head office which controls management. It will be the central point from which the different departments or branches are managed.

Working at Head Office

The Head Office of a big company may deal with enquiries for or from the Personnel Department, Buying Department, Accounts Department and so on. There may also be enquiries from outsiders to deal with – potential customers, competing organisations, or even the Press. As with the small company, you will still need to find out who does what. In this case, though, it is more likely to be a department rather than a single person. Again, too, you need to discover where you fit in. Something to bear in mind is that in a large central office, levels of responsibility tend to be strictly defined. You may need to get the authority of the next person up in the responsibility order before, say, you pass on a sales enquiry to the appropriate department, or even help yourself to some extra copy paper from the stationery cupboard.

Specialised departments

If you work in an office that provides a specialised service (it can be anything from medical records in a hospital to publicity in a food manufacturing firm), then your office will be providing a service (a) to other departments within the organisation, (b) to the Head Office of the organisation and (c) to outsiders. As well as being generally skilled in office work, and in dealing with people inside and outside the organisation, you will probably also need to 'add on' skills in particular aspects of the work, related to the activities of your department.

For example, in the Medical Records Department, you might well have to learn to use a computer to update medical information about patients, or access the appointments diaries of consultants so that you can send out recall cards to regular patients. Or if you join the publicity unit of a food manufacturing company, you may need to learn – and quickly – the names of food writers on newspapers, magazines, radio and television, so that if they should ring up for information about new products, you can put them in touch with your company's spokesperson on those products (otherwise the opportunity for publicity might be lost).

It could also be important to understand systems that enable you to pass information between people very quickly – everything from using the photocopier to print off urgent press releases to sending product samples by courier. Other examples of skills that could be important in specialised environments might be using a stopwatch for timing interviews in radio or television; planning and booking travel arrangements for an export manager; learning a word-processing system that enables you to 'personalise' a standard letter of enquiry for new business on behalf of an insurance company.

Branches

If you work in a branch office of a big organisation, you will have to abide by the regulations and deadlines of the parent company (i.e. all invoices to Head Office by 15th of the month) and, as usual, find out who does what, both in your own branch office and the Head Office of the organisation. However, the way in which work is managed in your own branch, and the procedure for handling enquiries may differ according to the size and location of your branch. Small units tend to be less formal, though staff have to tackle a wider range of jobs as a result.

If you are one of a dozen clerks in a big branch office in a city, your responsibilities are likely to be more closely defined than if you are one of two clerks in a branch office situated in a country town. All office workers need to be adaptable, but it is especially important to bear it in mind if you hope to make a career working for an organisation where promotion comes through moving locations. (This can be true in the Civil Service, in the National Health Service, in banks and building societies, for example.) Flexibility lets you make the most of your opportunities.

For instance, you might find that you are offered a promotion from a country office to one that involves supervising five clerks in a city branch. On the other hand, you might have the chance to be promoted to an administrative post in say, a cottage hospital or residential home, where you will handle most of the paperwork, having done well in a specialised administrative job in a big district health authority office.

Clients can be different in different environments too. In a big, crowded city, where people compete not only for jobs but for seats on trains and in cafés, clients (on the phone, or calling at the office in person) may be under pressure and expect to get swift, brief answers. They usually do not want to chat; in fact busy people may forget to be pleasant when they are rushed.

It is not necessarily true that in a small place or a small office the pace is slower and friendlier. But often the atmosphere is more informal and you may find that clients expect to be recognised and to exchange a few friendly remarks. They prefer to be known as Mr Jones or Mrs Smith, rather than 'Sir' or 'Madam' when you talk to them. Watch how people around you deal with enquirers or visitors and you will be able to adapt your approach to the circumstances.

Who does what?

First days in a new job are usually pretty awful. This is just as true if you are in the new job as General Manager, junior secretary or clerical assistant. For even at the top, you may only know a handful of the people you manage, and then only by their names and responsibilities. However, you will settle in more quickly and get more in the way of help if you make a real effort to match names and faces to their jobs as soon as you can.

Just as at a party, where you are whisked around being introduced to a lot of total strangers, so in the average office – the person appointed to be your guide and adviser for the first few days may gallop you through the assembled company and hope that you will recall everyone's name and background as required.

Very few of us can do this. So begin by being quite clear about the name of the person who is supervising you (write it down if you are not clear about the spelling) and what his or her job is.

Making contacts

The next important thing is to try and work out which other people in the office you are likely to have to deal with often. Think carefully about this. Eventually it will be important for you to know that

Ms Pacey is Assistant Marketing Manager (Publications) or that Mr Tew is Careers Officer (Higher Education). But in your first week the people you need to try to get to know are those in charge of the equipment or the services you may need to use. For example, it is probably important to know that the person who deals with the switchboard is called 'Jenny', that the boss's secretary is called 'Anthea' and that 'Mr Kops' is in charge of stationery. Find out, too, which people prefer to be called Mr or Miss or Mrs or Ms, and which prefer first names to be used. The etiquette of a particular office may be that the boss calls all the staff by their first names, but all the staff call him or her 'Mr/Ms' Jones. You may also have to adapt to a different etiquette where clients are concerned. 'Anthea' becomes 'Miss Smith' when you are taking a visitor through to wait in her office to see the manager. 'Jim' in the design office may become 'Mr Carter' or 'Jim Carter'. Again, watch and listen to the other office staff.

Seeking advice

If you are someone returning to work after a break, the new informality can be quite hard to grasp, particularly the way you have to switch your approach when dealing with different people. It does no harm to admit it, and to say to someone friendly that you are finding this aspect of work different – have they any tips for you? People usually like to share their expertise.

If you are working for a new small business, or even running your own office as part of setting up your own business, you can make the rules. Generally speaking, it is conventional to introduce yourself using your first name and your surname. On the phone you might say 'This is Betty Ling', or 'George Over speaking', but to address potential clients or say, suppliers, as Mr or Miss/Ms/Mrs. Older people brought up in traditional ways may not like the use of first names without invitation. It may be a bit awkward to say on the phone 'I would like to speak to – now is it Miss, or Mrs or Ms Johnson', but it is better than possibly causing offence by saying 'I would like to speak to Linda Johnson' and then receiving an icy reply 'This is *Mrs* Johnson. Who is that, please?' Mind you, you can still get it wrong. I once had to interview a university official who squashed me flat when I politely asked, 'Would you like to be described as Miss, Ms or Mrs?' 'Professor, thank you!' was her reply.

Recording information

When you are matching names to faces and jobs, you will find it is a good time to start what will eventually become an Office Notebook. To begin with, it will serve your purpose to make brief notes on a notepad you can keep in a pocket or handbag. They can cover everything from 'Mr Kops – runs stationery cupboard. Ask before 11 a.m.' to 'Couriers – always try Speedpost first, otherwise use Taxifast, Bike-along, Maximove, others in *Yellow Pages* phone book'.

Once you have settled in, you can start transferring these scrappy but useful notes into a neat, alphabetical index. It will be helpful if you are ever away sick, or for anyone who comes after you if you are promoted. Once the Office Notebook system is established, everyone will want to refer to it, including top management, intent on finding 'the name of that little Italian restaurant where they put on that marvellous meal for the clients from Manchester', or instructions on how to refill the photocopier when it runs out of paper.

Back to early days. As well as finding out who does what, which helps you to know where to go for advice or instructions, you also need to know:

Where you fit in

You may think you already know. After all, they told you at the interview. In the small firm, you have to help everybody. In the large firm, you have to help – well, at least all the people in your department, and perhaps later, outsiders. In the specialist department, you often serve both outside users *and* other departments in the organisation *and* the Head Office.

To be realistic, in most organisations, large and small, anyone new is often received very enthusiastically by busy people who may think, 'Oh, good. At last, someone to buy the milk for tea on the way in to work . . . take over reception so I can have a decent lunch hour . . . type the invoices . . . send out the reminder cards . . . water the rubber plant.' (*See Chapter 2 Planning and priorities*.)

When in doubt, write it out

Naturally you want to please everyone in your new environment, so there is a temptation to take on too much. If you should find this happening, take a deep breath, write down all the things you have been asked to do. If in doubt, *ask* your immediate superior or someone else you trust, which jobs are essential and which can be left for another time.

The next chapter deals with ways of getting your priorities right but once you see the work piling up, then, when you are new, it is always safer to ask where you should begin.

If for some reason there is no one to ask, combine common sense with your job description (as given to you at the interview). You have to take some responsibility for your decisions. It is no good saying 'But the job description says that as a medical secretary I type and file notes and make the appointments' when you are faced with a frantic patient saying that he must get a doctor to check his vaccination records *now* because he is flying to Africa on Friday! Common sense dictates that you should stop typing and filing and try to find someone to deal with him.

12

Learning the ropes

Whether you are straight from college, trained in the latest office systems; a 'returner' with years of experience to contribute to an office; a 'second jobber' confident because you have proved yourself already as a capable worker; or someone setting up his/her own office and therefore able to please yourself how it is run, there will still be plenty to learn.

Often it is not what seem to be huge tasks that are difficult. A great pile of enquiries may mean you have to stay late putting leaflets into envelopes but that is not the problem. Finding that you have run out of stamps and the post office has shut certainly is! Or it may be something like a frantic hunt for 10p pieces to put in the parking meter when the manager rushes in saying 'I've found a space, but I only had one 10p. Quick, who has change for a pound?' Or the manager's secretary, trying to catch the post, says 'Quickly, bring me an A5 envelope.' You know what A4 is, but *A5*?

These are all things you can decide to learn about for yourself. They may or may not be part of your job description. Your role may be to type the envelopes, not order different sizes. Someone else may run the petty cash book, or be in charge of buying stamps. But you can still ask tactful questions . . . 'Do you want me to go to the post office and get stamps for these leaflets if they have to go out tonight?' or 'You know when I have to call in a courier? Well, what's the procedure for getting the money to pay the courier company?' or 'When the photocopier broke down, and you had to use the one in the post office, did they give you change for it, or do we have to keep a float for that?'

Ask at the right moment

Obviously you cannot ask all these questions at once! There is no surer way of exasperating fellow workers than constantly interrupting them with questions and problems. But as opportunities occur, try to find out what systems are in operation, where things are kept, which suppliers are favoured. All this is information for the Office Notebook.

To sum up

When you are settling into your office job, you should find out:

- What the organisation does
- Who your office serves
- What your job involves
- Who can advise you
- What facilities you can use
- Which extra skills will be useful

. . . and you should start your own <u>Office</u> <u>Notebook</u>.

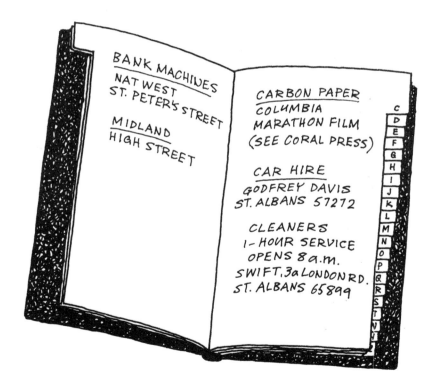

2 Planning and priorities

- Where do you fit in to the office routine?
- Can you work out a practical timetable for your own tasks?
- What about emergencies, absences, equipment breakdown – can you keep going?

First days in a new office are always difficult whether you are joining an established team with its own system or setting up a system for handling the office work of your own business.

It does take time to sort out an order of priorities for the jobs to be done. Even then, you will probably want to adapt your system as you go along. Once you have decided on an order of importance for each task, you can start working on a plan to make sure each job is completed by the due date. It needs to be clearly set out so that everyone involved in the work will understand what they have to do. There should also be a system of checking to guarantee that things still get done if the person who is supposed to handle a particular task should be away ill or on holiday.

That is the ideal. But how do you make a start, bearing in mind that if you are starting a new office job in someone else's organisation, you have to learn their routine, or if you are setting up your own firm, you have to create a routine?

What's to be done?

You cannot decide an order of priorities until you know what needs to be done, so in your first few days, write down what you have been told to do – or the tasks that crop up if you are self-employed. Do the work involved as well as you can in the time available, but if you find yourself getting behind, at this stage it is sensible to ask for advice on what to do. You do not really know enough about the work to sort out priorities for yourself. As and when you have time (and it will not necessarily be as you do each job) try and make a note that will later tell you how important it proved; how long it took; and who gave it to you.

NB For self-employed people, this does not just mean when the task came from the taxman, vatman or DHSS. Some clients do prove to be more trouble than the income they bring in. At first it is tempting to

15

take every scrap of work you are offered. But in time, you will have to decide which jobs are profitable and which are not. Even in the early days, you could find it fairly easy to identify the clients who are forever ringing up or writing or changing their minds!

Why routine is important

In someone else's office, you may not be able to pick and choose who you work for, but as the weeks go by, you will begin to realise which of the regular tasks have to take priority. To give you one example, anything to do with money coming in is usually a priority. If your organisation does not send out invoices by a certain date, the money is not likely to arrive for work done in time to be cleared by the bank so that you can be paid.

Of course this is a simplification. In a large profitable firm, the late arrival of a few bills is not going to mean that the office staff have to wait for their salaries. All the same, firms do not stay profitable long if the financial side is disorganised, so it is quite usual to have a specific date by which invoices must be dispatched each month. With some kinds of business, the invoice is sent with the goods. To the person who has to type invoices, this regular task may be seen as very boring but it is work on which the organisation's income depends.

Invoice preparation, typing and dispatch is an example of a regular task that has to be fitted into a schedule. Maintaining stocks of stationery and other day-to-day supplies is another. It is less likely to be organised in such a way that the order for fresh supplies has to be made at a particular time of the month, though big firms with a central stationery store may have such a system. In an organisation of average size or, of course, if you are self-employed, it is more a question of keeping an eye on supplies to make sure you do not risk running out of regularly-used items. This might be something to check on the same day each week – looking out for a time when you are less rushed.

Planning your own routine

Then there are the irregular, but very important, routine tasks that deserve the 'as soon as possible' description. For instance, suppose potential customers write in for a leaflet that describes your products,

16

service or organisation. This may not be an urgent task, but it is certainly an important one. We are all pleased to get a quick response to any enquiry we may make. In a well-organised office, there could well be a system whereby leaflets are kept in envelopes ready for addressing beside a pad on which a note of their dispatch date and the potential clients' names can be jotted down at the time, ready to transfer to a more permanent record of enquiry at a convenient time in the week.

Invoicing – stock control – sales literature dispatch. These are three examples of the sorts of tasks that might need to be done on a fairly regular basis in a commercial office.

In a professional office, for example, a doctor's surgery – the same kind of importance might be placed on sending monthly returns to the district health authority; keeping stocks of all the different forms needed to ask for hospital tests to be carried out; reminding patients to attend a particular clinic.

Who gets priority?

The most accomplished and experienced office worker can be flustered by conflicting demands to do that urgent piece of work in the first couple of weeks of a new job. Even someone who is regarded as an 'administrator' with staff to whom she or he can delegate tasks needs time to discover who is normally responsible for maintaining the holiday lists or whose work has priority with regard to using the photocopier.

Newcomers to office life can feel quite bewildered by the conflicting demands on their time, so it is as well to recognise that other people's attitudes can often mislead you into thinking something is very urgent when it might be a task that can wait.

'That's not fair!', you may feel. Probably not, but part of coping with office life is to recognise that other people want to succeed in their work too. They want to impress the boss with their efficiency and speed, so, seeing an eager newcomer who can help them with some important project (well, important to them), they will press you into service. Similarly, if you are self-employed, every customer is out to get the best service possible.

In time, you will learn both about the personalities of people you work with or for, and how when Mr Jones says 'Now this work is very important. I'd like it done today', what it actually means is that he would *like* it done today . . . and when you have got a bit more experience, you will know it can wait until tomorrow. On the other hand, when Mrs Smith says 'This letter needs to catch tonight's post', she means that it *must* catch tonight's post. Only time will tell who panics easily and also which people may understate their case. As always, when in doubt, ask.

Incidentally, in doing your asking, you do not have to seem either inefficient or unco-operative. 'Can you advise me . . . ' is a tactful phrase to start with. 'Can you advise me if I should do this before Mrs Smith's urgent letter to the publishers? . . . Can you advise me? I don't know how long it takes to photocopy 50 leaflets and Mr Jones said he'd like them in the post tonight, so which job shall I do first?' should get a helpful response.

Keeping up to date

As you settle into your job, you will learn about the ebb and flow of work in the office and be able to look ahead and know that, say, Friday afternoon is a quiet time when you can catch up with less urgent jobs – or get ahead with some of Monday's work.

In most offices, there are times in the month – often after the busiest period – when the pace of work slows right down. This is the sort of time when you can reorganise the filing system or enter the hand-written addresses you have gathered at a busy time into their right place on the computer. Make notes of non-urgent but useful jobs you can turn to when the pressure eases.

According to the business that you are in, you might want to spend time in the library finding out what trade reference books and magazines they keep; compare different types of office equipment for value and cost of operation; tackle a long-standing problem – anything from finding a reliable courier service to tracking down a phone system whereby you can record quotations given over the phone.

Planning your time

Office equipment shops offer a tempting array of wall charts, year planners, calendars and diaries to customers in search of the perfect system for planning office work. Each has its values. For instance, everyone will find it valuable to know when individuals will be away on holiday. This ensures that vital meetings are not arranged for times when people who should attend will be absent and it helps you look ahead and reschedule tasks that fall due when someone will be away, or reassign the work to someone who can act as a stand-in. Year planners are very useful for indicating holiday absences, important annual events like exhibitions or regular board meetings. A small organisation may find that there is space for reminders about delivery dates, checking stock or sales trips.

Master diary

But however useful a year planner may be, people cannot keep rushing in and out of the office where it is displayed, or indeed, taking it off the wall to refer to when they are answering a telephone enquiry. (Variations, like a month planner or week planner may be one solution, as is duplicating the year planner.) But most people find there also needs to be a central office diary in which all appointments, meetings and absences are noted.

With a small company where there are just a handful of employees, this can be an ordinary 'day-at-a-time' diary kept up to date by say, the manager's secretary, but stored in reception near the switchboard. This location has several advantages. First of all, when people phone in and ask to speak to Mr Lewis or Ms Parker, the person who answers the telephone can check quickly to see if they are available. Then again, when visitors are expected, if their name and expected arrival time is noted in the master diary, the person on reception can greet them. It gives a very good impression if when someone walks through the door at five minutes to eleven, the receptionist behind the desk can say 'Mr Carter? Mrs Joseph is expecting you. Please do sit down and I'll let her know you're here.'

'Let me check the diary'

The master diary can be consulted by people who are out of the office. Salespeople, for example, can ring in to check whether the company will be having a stand at a certain exhibition, so that they can tell their clients. A manager who has forgotten his own personal diary or appointments book can call the switchboard and check on the date of a board meeting. Someone from another office who wants to arrange a meeting for a number of busy people (all of whom may have to travel some distance to the event) can ring in and perhaps get a choice of dates still free according to the master diary.

If it is your responsibility to keep a master diary of this kind, make sure you have the authority to check individuals' desk diaries, and to enter (in pencil until firmly agreed) the time of any proposed meeting or assignments. Such 'pencilled in' material should appear both in the master diary and the diary of the individual concerned.

'May I check the spelling?'

One other important point – such information must be *legible*. Most of us think we write neatly, but it is sensible to print names in block capitals. The same applies to addresses: CITY HOSPITAL, KIMBERLEY CLINIC, or L'APERITIF RESTAURANT. It is often a good idea to get people to spell their names, and you can do it with the simplest of names. 'Is that Smith with an "i" in the middle or Smythe with a "y".' Getting people to spell out their names can avoid great hassles later, too, with filing. I always have to say, 'That's Korving, starting with a "k" . . .' and even then, if I am watching someone write it down, they will still try to start it off with a 'c'!

With a large organisation, the same kind of master diary can be kept on a departmental basis. It is customary for the secretary to the person in charge to have the responsibility of making entries in the master diary and to deal with enquiries relating to it.

'I'll confirm that date'

In hospitals, diaries are frequently augmented by computerised appointments systems. The clinic clerk can call up a particular consultant's clinic day for a week, a month, three months ahead and enter a patient's appointment. This information is cross-referenced; the patient gets a letter or a card confirming the day, time and consultant. The consultant gets a printed or typewritten list of appointments made in good time to collect any notes or test reports needed for each patient.

Work sheets

The year planner and the master diary system are invaluable for groups of people working together, but most office workers need their own diary for events that concern them personally – meetings, exhibitions, holidays. Once you know enough about your range of responsibilities to start sorting out those that are regular, it is helpful to devise a personal work sheet, to keep by you on your desk (with a photocopy you can fold up and keep in a pocket or handbag, just in case your sheet goes missing). It is useful, too, to have your work sheet with you if you happen to be out on company business – you can see just when you are free and when time has been committed for a particular job.

I use a sheet of lined A4 paper with a left-hand margin, heading it with the month and year. In the margin, I write 'Tues.1st, Weds.2nd, Thurs.3rd', and so on. I indicate where the weekends come with a black underlining right across the page for Saturday and Sunday dates. (This is less because I do not work at weekends – in practice, I often do – but because most offices are shut over the weekend.) I use the same black underlining for bank holidays, when offices will be shut.

Then, I write in on the appropriate line any event that occupies a day or part of a day. As I am a journalist, copy dates (the dates on which articles or book copy have to be delivered) are important. So are press conferences which are held to publicise products, services or developments – in the case of the work I do, new examinations, new courses, new careers guides. I have to enter appointments I may have made to interview people and dates when I have to complete official returns – for VAT, for instance. Finally, there are personal items – maybe there is a TV documentary I want to watch because it has some bearing on what I write about, or it could be a family birthday.

Quick reference coding

Because it is useful to take in at a glance what is happening in any particular week, I use colour coding on my work sheets: I write in the information and then use a coloured marker pen to highlight the kind of work involved. Green indicates anything that involves going out of the office – an interviewing session, a press show, or even a dental appointment. If it means going out, it is 'Green for Go'.

SUN. 1ST	
MON . 2ND	BANK HOLIDAY
TUE . 3RD	COPY DUE / 15CO
WED. 4 TH	VET 5.15
THUR. 5TH	SOCIAL WORK CONFERENCE 10.00 AM LONDON
FRI. 6TH	PCAS VIDEO 11.45 AM LONDON
SAT. 7TH	
SUN. 8TH	
MON. 9TH	CH. IV
TUE. 10TH	OPEN UNIV CONFERENCE 11AM LONDON CH. III
WED. 11TH	MOTHER'S BIRTHDAY

For crucial completion dates, whether they refer to work that must be delivered on time or official returns that are due, I use a red marker pen. 'Red for Danger' seems appropriate since I will be in hot water if I miss any of these vital dates.

Yellow is the colour I use to indicate personal matters – the TV programme I want to view, the family birthday, a visit from an old friend. I see this as 'Yellow for Sunshine' because it is something to look forward to, rather than a responsibility.

You may need more colours to code your personal work sheet. Marker pens come in all colours, including blue, orange and purple. In a busy commercial office, you would probably want a colour to identify meetings that take place on your own premises. Orange is a welcoming colour and might be ideal. Maybe there is a task that has to be done regularly that makes you feel blue, or a rather grand inspection that takes place every so often that you think deserves the royal purple.

After twenty-five years of trying all kinds of planning systems, I can promise you this one works really well. You will probably find that office colleagues copy it as it is so easy to see a looming important date indicated by 'Red for Danger', or spot the fact that you (or the manager you work for) seems to be spending a great deal of time outside the office with all those 'Green for Go' markers, so no wonder the paperwork is piling up!

Contingency planning

Once you have sorted out which tasks need to be undertaken regularly and established an order of priority for them, so that you can plan the work, you need to start thinking what you will do if someone throws a spanner into it! What if the computer goes wrong? Suppose there is a postal strike? Suppose you fall ill and have to take a month off? What would happen?

Now as it happens, I have chosen three things that have affected me and my small business in my time, so I do know how devastating the effects can be. Any one of these events could finish off a small business, and they can cause a great deal of trouble and inconvenience to a large one. Any plan for running an office should include a range of things you can do if trouble strikes and makes it impossible to do the work in the way you usually do.

Equipment first

The smaller the firm, the more crucial it is to have a reliable servicing arrangement for your typewriter, computer, telephone answering machine, or photocopier. When you cannot go to another department for help, you must be able to call on a servicing system that provides immediate repair and/or a substitute piece of equipment. If you are a very small firm, and you really cannot afford to commit yourself to a contract providing servicing, you must find a system of working that is going to mean you can cope even if your equipment does give up.

Do not put all your vital information on the computer if a breakdown might mean you cannot get at it. Use a card index as well. And if you use your computer for word-processing too, be sure you have contacts with a local typing bureau where in emergency you could get letters, invoices or reports typed.

Again, find out where the nearest commercial photocopying service is offered. Few things are more likely to send your blood pressure soaring than discovering that the post office's photocopier is out of order on the very day that you desperately need to use it, or that the one in the public library may be working, but as the library closes on Thursday afternoons, you cannot reach it.

If the telephone answering machine goes wrong and you have to

wait for a repair, can you use people to answer? How much do you know about British Telecom's facilities for having calls transferred to another number in such an emergency? What are the situations in which this can be arranged and how long does it take? This is the sort of information to copy into the Office Notebook referred to in Chapter 1, and there are other useful additions you can make.

One of the most valuable tasks you can tackle on a quiet day is to walk around the district where your office is situated and find out exactly what services there are on the doorstep (and get price lists if you can). Do not limit yourself to office services. If your hand slips when you are taking a tray of coffee and biscuits in to the board meeting and you splash coffee over the Managing Director's suit, the fact that you know a one-hour cleaner may yet save your reputation. Or in some emergency, you may be asked to arrange refreshments for a group of people working late. If there is not a handy canteen, which of the local cafés or takeaways can supply food suitable for a buffet meal? At the 'upper end' of the market, do you know your local restaurants? Can you suggest somewhere to take a guest who is a vegetarian?

Alternatives

Transport facilities are also something you need to be knowledgeable about in terms of contingency planning. Cars can break down, trains can be cancelled. It is very helpful to be able to suggest alternative ways of travel ('What about the shuttle to Edinburgh?' or 'Shall I try for a seat on an express coach?' 'Do you want me to hire a car for you?') and to be capable of finding overnight accommodation when required. Travel agencies can usually solve transport problems but may not always book hotels, particularly in smaller places. By contacting the appropriate national tourist board (English, Welsh, Scottish, Northern Ireland) you can get from them the address of the regional or local tourist information office for the place concerned to advise you on accommodation.

Using your initiative

What about unexpected hazards such as strikes? Well, if it is a national shutdown of postal or transport services, at least everyone else is in the same boat. Local strikes or 'work to rule' incidents are much harder to cope with. Get some kind of communication going if you can. Companies take all sorts of action to try and cope with hold-ups of this kind. For instance, it is by no means unusual when a particular district has its postboxes sealed, for the organisation to collect all the mail and drive it to a district ten or fifteen miles away where the post is being collected and forwarded. Organisations may cope with transport strikes by staggering times of work, so that instead of getting trapped in a jam during the rush, people work unconventional shifts for a short period. It may be possible for some work to be done at home and for very urgent written or diagrammatic material to be transmitted over the telephone using the fax system. (*See Chapter 5 Information flow and retrieval.*)

The other 'contingency' I gave as an example is illness, and how well people can cope on your behalf (or how you can cope with someone else's work), depends on how efficiently it has been planned. If you operate the work sheet system, someone else should be able to see at a glance what you have planned to do. Even if yours is a one-person business, the work sheet and diaries should provide enough clues for your files to be searched for addresses, and appointments cancelled with explanations given. If you have a partner or if you work in a larger organisation, it is possible that someone can take over from you. But without your plans and priorities clearly set out and easily accessible, chaos could result.

To sum up

When planning your work to deal with priorities, duties, and contingencies, you should find out:

- What work must be done by specific dates (and why)
- What work must be done at regular intervals (and how often)
- What to do when two tasks seem equally urgent
- What work you may fit in to suit yourself
- Which office charts and diaries can help you
- How to plan your personal work schedule
- Which outside sources can be useful
- How to establish a system that copes with contingencies

3 Telephone skills

- How do you sound on the phone?
- Friendly? Polite? Keen to help?
- Can you gather information by telephone?
- Take down important messages accurately?
- Cope with an answering machine?

A flair for working on the telephone is one of the most valuable attributes you can bring to office work. When you use it to respond to calls, the way you answer callers conveys an immediate impression of your organisation's efficiency and the pleasant way they can expect to be treated. When you use the telephone for outgoing calls, your approach can convey courtesy, confidence and appreciation of information you are given so that people go out of their way to be helpful and co-operative.

In business, the purpose of the telephone is to provide a bridge between the company and the client. Alas, all too often, it is a barrier. Examples of good practice are rare but remembered.

Making the caller welcome

There is the reassuring response of our local medical practice: 'Good morning. This is the Health Centre', from a calm, friendly voice which suggests that the entire team is waiting to make you better.

Then there is the encouraging approach of those BBC secretaries who say 'Hello! You're through to Antonia Rolfe's office.' Again, this makes you feel your call is expected and they are glad to confirm that you have reached the right place.

British Rail Euston's General Enquiry Service has impressed me on several occasions with different operators, so it must be in their training. They say something like, 'British Rail Euston. Can I help you?' They answer queries in a considered and friendly way that shows you that they really want to help and not just get rid of you as soon as possible.

On one occasion, I arrived at the Business & Technician Education Council's offices, I sat opposite the reception desk and heard the receptionist answer the telephone again and again, each time sounding pleased to respond to the call, 'BTEC. Can I help you?' It was not so much *what* she said as her tone of voice that showed she was really keen to be helpful.

First impressions like these are a marvellous advertisement for the organisation they represent. They also put callers in a good mood for later conversations. Yet how many times have you rung a company only to be greeted by: 'Bent 'n Smi–i–i–ths, g'morning', dragged out in a bored drawl, or 'Phelps & Dew!' snapped at you so that you are taken aback and so hesitate to ask what you want.

'Are you still there, operator?'

As for second impressions, everyone has their own horror story about being put through to the wrong extension and then getting lost on the return to the switchboard, being made to recite their entire requirements to the switchboard operator (often at peak charge time) and then being told that the person wanted is on another telephone number. Or being told to hold on . . . and on . . . and on . . . until you get tired of saying 'Is anyone there?' and ring off, having wasted both time and money and lost your temper.

Then there is the 'Well, I don't know' fraternity. You ask to speak to Mr Elliot and he is out. 'When do you expect him back?' (They don't know.) 'Is there someone else who could answer a question about the product?' (They don't know that, either.) 'Is there a good time when I might ring to speak to Mr Elliot?' (You'd think they lived on a different planet. They don't know that either.) Moreover, all too often, it is not even 'don't know' but 'dunno', in the tone of someone who could not care less.

The only worse reaction I have come across is on the occasions when you are simply informed that Mr Elliot is out – after which the call is cut off before you can make any comment at all!

Using 'want' power

Yet strangely, the same inadequate telephone personalities may be perfectly able to chat on the phone with friends, make clear enquiries about when the big film starts at the cinema, or follow up a newspaper advertisement for a second-hand TV. If they have to report a fire, flood or accident, they are also quite capable of getting the message across. Only at work does telephone boredom set in. If it is not nipped in the bud, it can serioulsy damage their career prospects.

Using willpower

There are some people who are genuinely scared of dealing with phone calls. Most of us would be sympathetic with a new employee who says he or she has very little experience of using a phone and certainly not in an office.

If, for example, you have not had a telephone at home, you may see the office phone as yet another tricky piece of equipment to learn, like the typewriter or the computer. There it sits, threatening to ring, and what is more, you know that other people in the office will be able to hear how well or badly you cope. (With the typewriter at least you could not be overheard going wrong.) But telephone skills can be acquired quickly and easily, and before you even start to absorb techniques by listening to other people on the phone, there is a golden rule to put into practice. Use it every time you answer the phone and you will sound pleasant and confident, even if you are rather apprehensive.

Treat the telephone as a person

It makes no difference whether the caller on the other end of the phone is in the next-door office or 500 miles away, you still get the best results if you behave as if you are talking to them face to face. Many firms providing sessions in the use of telephone techniques tell you to smile each time you answer the phone so that you will automatically adopt a friendly attitude.

I think this is probably a counsel of perfection. Most of us can manage to be polite when the telephone rings for the fourth time in the middle of a tricky piece of work, but giving a cheery smile is rather too much to expect. (No doubt we will have to learn to do it when the videophone arrives.) Accepting that a jolly smile is not always possible, using the same clear and pleasant phrase can become an automatic response.

On the other hand, you should not feel you have to put on a different voice or a posh accent when you answer the telephone. You would not use a strange accent if you were talking face to face with your colleagues or clients, so do not change your voice on the telephone: it will sound unnatural, and you will not be able to keep it up.

Accents can be a plus factor

You need to speak clearly of course, but that is not the same as changing your accent. In practice, a regional accent can both be very pleasant and help people to remember you.

Being a Devonian, I tend to respond to a West Country accent very warmly. Voices with lots of light and shade are attractive – there is the Welsh lilt and the Scottish burr. And I had not realised until a caller told me one day that her cheerful voice (which seemed to 'lift' at the end of every sentence) was a Birmingham accent. 'Fancy someone liking my Brummie accent,' she said. But her speech was always clear and lively, and that is something we all appreciate when we have to take down information from a telephone caller.

The Midlands accent is one in which you hear the ends of words, and perhaps that is what makes for clarity. People from India, Pakistan and Bangladesh also speak in a precise way that makes them easy to understand on the telephone. If you listen to phone-in programmes on the radio, you will see that it is being able to speak distinctly rather than in a high-class drawl that makes for easy understanding – vital in business. Saying the whole of a word, e.g. 'train*ing*' rather than 'trainun' and making sure you keep your voice up, rather than letting it fade away at the end of a sentence helps people hear what you mean.

How do you sound?

Have you ever listened to your voice on a tape recorder? 'That's not *me*!' most people cry. It is true that a poor quality tape recorder is not likely to reproduce your voice very well, and also it can make a difference when you are self-consciously speaking into a tape recorder operated by someone else. However, if you can spend some time practising on your own with a tape recorder, it can be a real help in developing your speaking voice and correcting any weak points. You can begin by reading short paragraphs from a newspaper and then playing them back.

Do not be too critical of your style – you are not trying to copy Michael Aspel or Sue Cook. Just listen to see if you are clear and if you sound interested in what you are reading.

This practice will be most effective if you pick out newspaper items that you do not personally find very interesting. When you respond to a business call, you will not always be answering queries on things you find particularly fascinating. If you can make yourself sound interested when you are reading a dull newspaper report, you are ready for the next stage, which is to record different ways in which you might answer the phone, and play them back.

Rehearsing your response

'Hello' can be one of the most difficult words of all to begin with – experienced broadcasters will tell you it is hard not to sound over-hearty or coy. It is often easier to begin with 'Good morning' (or Good afternoon if that is appropriate), or to say 'This is . . . ', followed by the organisation's name.

Incoming calls

Many organisations have a specific phrase they want you to use when you answer the phone. If your company insists that you answer simply with their name, i.e. 'Gammon, Hambone, Porkpie and Brawn' there is not a lot you can do about it. That, at least, is quite a memorable name; it would be more of a problem if you had to answer 'Smith, Jones & Green'.

The reason for trying to precede the organisation's name with a phrase like 'Good morning' is that often the first word or so of an answer may not be very clear. It is sometimes because the person answering is dealing with another call at the same time, so may not be speaking directly into the mouthpiece of the phone. It may be because they are not concentrating entirely on the call which may have interrupted some other work.

Then there is the possibility that the caller may be about to ring off – if you have been delayed in responding (you may have been in another office), then just as you do pick up the phone after ten rings, the caller may be saying 'Well, they're clearly not there' and the words 'not there' could overlap the 'Gammon, Hambone' or 'Smith, Jones' part of the reply.

Greetings

Using a greeting is helpful. If you say 'Good morning! Smith, Jones & Green', it does not matter if the 'Good morning' gets lost. Or you might try out: 'This is Smith, Jones & Green.' You might decide to put the emphasis on the particular office. Then you might say 'Smith, Jones & Green, *Buying* Department.' You could also try 'You're through to *Accounts*, Smith, Jones & Green.' Just a word or two preceding the

32

name or location that you are identifying is a good idea.

What about giving the telephone number? If you have a one-person business, it is probably a good idea. Use the name of the location – Leicester or St Albans or Bradford – followed by the number. A string of figures is hard to absorb but naming your town could be very helpful to the caller who may only have been given the dialling code and not know where your business is located. After the number you can give either your own name or the business name you have chosen 'Dozy Duvets' or 'Beady Eye Detectives.'

Identifying callers

Also in one-person businesses, you will expect to have to handle every call that comes in, whether or not it is convenient for you, unless you get an answering machine (*see page 36*). If you are running an office for someone else, you may be given specific instructions about the sorts of calls to put through, or the questions that should be asked before you put a caller through. In some companies, you are left to use your own judgement.

Always have a couple of pens and a notepad by the telephone – you need *two* pens in case one runs out just as you are taking down an important message, and note each call that comes in.

Your caller will usually either ask you a question like 'Does your company supply bacon offcuts?' or 'May I make an appointment to see your packaging buyer?' or ask to be put through to an individual, either by name 'Mrs Lester' or 'the person who deals with purchasing, please, and by the way who is that?'

Learn to be helpful

In the early weeks of a new office job, you can usually find out what the preferred policy is for dealing with enquiries. Are you expected to give certain kinds of information yourself? With regard to enquiries about items sold by your firm you may be expected to say 'May I have your name and address so that I can put a price list/catalogue/brochure in the post today to you.' Or with regard to the appointment, the policy may be to say, 'I'll put you through to the Purchasing Department about that; who shall I say is calling?' As for giving names, most companies are quite happy for you to name the person responsible, but may instruct you to suggest that the caller writes for an appointment rather than rings or calls in at the office.

Keep callers informed

Suppose it is left to you to decide what you should do when people ring your office with requests to speak to your seniors, or for information that you are not sure you should give out. The first thing to do is to show that you are taking action. In the case of someone who wants to speak to the manager, you can say 'I'll check and see if he's available' – and do that. It can be helpful if you are able to tell a caller you have to turn away just when a call might be more convenient: 'If you'd like to ring tomorrow between 10 and 12 noon, Mrs Theaker should be available then.' In the case of the enquirer who wants to know about the company's products or services, you would normally say 'I'll transfer you to our Sales Department. One moment please.' Then, with the caller on 'hold', let the Sales Department know that the call is coming through. If the department is engaged, tell the caller so, and again, suggest a different time to call.

On the question of giving out names, if you have no one to advise you as to whether this is allowed or not, you can often deal with the difficulty by asking a question. For instance, with the caller who wanted to know the name of the Purchasing Manager, you could say 'We have several different people handling purchasing; can you let me know what it's about, so I can suggest the right person.' This at least lets you direct computer software salespeople to the person in charge of office supplies, and food packaging materials sales people to the production buyer.

Notes of telephone calls

Even if it is only a very brief note, it aids efficiency to jot down the name of each caller and their organisation. At the end of the day, someone may say to you 'I suppose you don't remember the name of that chap from the packaging firm. I've made a note of the company, but I can't read my writing – was it *Harker* or *Hacker*?' If you have had a very busy day answering the phone and consequently you have not managed to get on with some other jobs you have to do, it is also evidence of all the interruptions you have had!

When noting names and addresses, check them back. Say something like 'That's Mr Lygon . . . is that L Y G O N? . . . and you're at Speciality Soups, 76 Luton Road, Nutfield?' It might be Ligon with an 'i', and he could be at 76 Ludon Road – checking will prevent an error in writing.

If your caller wants to speak to someone who is not available for any reason, your note should be more detailed. Get the telephone number of Speciality Soups as well as the address. Note the time of their call. Add any information that will be useful to the person who will have to reply, such as, 'Rang to ask if we supplied bacon offcuts.'

If there is no policy about dealing with calls for individuals who cannot or will not take them, you must combine being pleasant to the caller with being loyal to your employer. This is often solved by telling a little white lie, but if you cannot bring yourself to say that Mrs Jones is in a meeting when you know quite well she is working on her computer forecast, the phrase 'not available' is both useful and truthful.

On the other hand, you may have to back it up with an alternative time for the caller to contact Mrs Jones. It is difficult to keep your cool when you have had Mrs Jones hissing in your ear 'Say I'm out, at a meeting, off sick, *anything*', but you can try: 'Mrs Jones won't be available at all today, Mr Green, and she prefers people to write in, rather than phone. If you'd like to write in, mark the letter URGENT and I will draw it to her attention as soon as it arrives.' This gets you out of a difficult situation, and if Mrs Jones then wants to turn the caller away having had the letter, that is her responsibility.

Would you like to wait?

What if you think Mrs Jones would like to speak to the caller but her line is continually engaged? Be truthful, and keep reassuring the caller if he or she decides to wait in the hope of getting through. Sympathise by saying 'I know how irritating it must be to have to wait like this. Are you sure you wouldn't like to ring later today?' If the caller continues to hold on, tell Mrs Jones about this long wait when she finally finishes the other conversation. It could make her less impatient when having to deal with another phone call immediately after finishing the previous one.

Taking messages

There are three things to remember about taking messages. First, read the message back to the person giving it, and check that you have names, places and times right. Then, write the message out neatly, ideally on a removable sticky message label which you can attach to the telephone or desk of the person for whom it is intended. Finally, and often forgotten, check to see that it has been received and acted upon. The person who asked you to pass on the message may ring again. It will be embarrassing for the company if you have to admit that, though you passed on the message, it is still there gathering dust because you have discovered the person involved is away sick or on holiday. When you are checking to see that the message has been received, if you do find out that the person is away, ask someone in authority what you should do about the call.

Outgoing calls

It sounds elementary to suggest that you should decide why you are making the call, but every day hundreds of people who are faced with an answering machine suddenly discover that they do not know! When they find they have to leave a message so that they can be called back, they replace the receiver in a hurry because they cannot summarise their requirements in a brief message.

Until you are very confident about your telephone skills, it is worth making a note of who you are calling, what you want to find out, and why. Then, if you are answered by a machine, this will be invaluable in devising your own message to leave. If you are not, it will make your questions clearer and more liable to produce an equally clear answer.

You might be asked to contact the secretary of an executive in another company who is being asked to a meeting, to fix a time that will be convenient. In this case, you need to begin with information about times that would be convenient in your office. The secretary at the other end cannot be very helpful if you do not know whether Tuesday afternoon or Thursday morning would be possibilities.

You will probably need to know the purpose of the meeting, too. Just 'a meeting' is pretty vague. 'A meeting with our Creative Team to discuss the Bacon Puffs promotion' is much better. You need to know how soon you want an answer about the time of the meeting. Suppose you ring and discover that the executive concerned is away at a conference? His secretary may be able to check his diary and see which times appear to be free, but you do need to know the latest date by which you can be advised when he can attend for a meeting.

Again, suppose you are asked to find out details of trains from London to St Helens and back . . . and 'Can I do it in a day?' Before you start checking timetables and talking to British Rail or the travel agency, you need some information about how long the traveller expects to stay in St Helens. Will it do if he just has a couple of hours for a meeting? Does he have to be there for a lunch? In which case, not only is it likely to be a very early start, but the cost will increase, as cheap return fares usually only operate after 9.30 a.m. Is the office in St Helens near the railways station? (This is a trick question; there are two stations.)

Justify your query

Executives asking office staff to tackle these kinds of tasks for them do not always take kindly to having to give chapter and verse, so sit down and think carefully about the sorts of questions that might be important, make a note of them, and then pick your moment for asking them. That way the answers will not take long and you will win approval for initiative.

In dealing with outsiders on behalf of someone in your office, it is usually best to say so. People will understand if you say 'I've been asked to find out (whatever it is) for Mrs Jones' and then have to refer back to find out if 9 a.m. on Thursday is a possibility, or whether Mrs Jones can be at Euston by 7.45 to catch a train to Liverpool for St Helens. On the other hand, if someone spends ages tracing information for you, and you then say, 'Well, I'll have to ring you back because it's not for me, you see', they could well feel they have wasted time because you have not the authority to make an appointment or book a rail ticket.

Can you advise me?

When you are making a phone call in search of information and you really do not know who to ask for, honesty pays off. Whether it is ICI, the DHSS or the Chartered Institute of Building Societies, the person who answers their phone will probably be someone rather like you, glad to help if they can as long as your requirements are clear.

I often have to ring organisations in search of people who can give me information for articles or broadcasts, and when I say simply 'I'm looking for someone who can give me details of distance-learning courses in estate agency work', or 'I don't know who to ask for, but I understand that there's a scheme whereby your university takes people with arts A-levels for engineering degrees,' invariably I'm passed on to the right person.

This system can be particularly helpful to remember for self-employed people. If, say, you are in the business of manufacturing personalised presents – anything from coffee mugs to knitted ponchos – and you want to arrange to show your samples to big stores, the person on the switchboard may be the very person to help you by telling you whether you should approach a Central Buying Department, or the Giftwear Buyer, or China and Glass Buyer/Fashion Buyer respectively.

Officials (tax, national insurance, council and so on) can be approached in the same way and in my experience, have just the same kind of helpful person answering their telephones.

Speak after the tone

If you are among the many people who hate and fear using answering machines, take heart. If you are going self-employed, or if at any stage in the future, you might want to set up your own business, the dear old answering machine will be your right hand. Not only will it retrieve possible clients and keep existing customers aware of your attention when you really *are* out of the office, but when you have some crucial project to complete (like your VAT return) and you must have a respite from the constantly ringing telephone, you can put a message on your answering machine to take calls until you are free to talk to people.

Many organisations which offer a 24-hour service use answering machines to redirect callers to a firm or individual who can give immediate attention. For example, our local veterinary practice can produce a veterinary surgeon to make a house call, see an animal at the surgery or talk over symptoms on the phone, 24-hours a day, seven days a week. Their machine answers calls with 'This is the Veterinary Hospital. To contact the veterinary surgeon on duty, please telephone such and such a number' – all you need.

In a company there may be a longer standard message, 'This is Davies, Howie and Cavender. The office is closed until 9 a.m. on Monday morning, but if you leave your name and telephone number, we will contact you as soon as we reopen.'

In a very small business, and particularly in a business operated from your home you should beware of inviting burglars by implying you are out. You might say something like 'You're through to (give the number) Dozy Duvets. Would you be kind enough to leave your name and phone number so we can call you back as there is no one available in the office to take calls at present. Please speak after the tone.' Obviously you may want a message with a bit more sparkle and character to it, depending on the business you are in. Always try to sound really friendly, not like Robbie the Robot, and you will find people *do* leave messages.

Talking back to the machine

Treat it like a person, and talk as you would on an ordinary phone call. It is fine to say 'Hello. This is Amanda Asquith of Amanda's Design, telephone 0272 00727. Can you give me a call back, please? This message timed at 11.08 on Wednesday 11th May. Thank you.'

If in doubt, do not record a message you are unhappy about. Put the phone down, write out your message, read it over so that it says all that is needed and then ring the answering machine again to record it. Yes, this is a bit expensive for your employer (or an extra few pence on the bill, if you are self-employed). But it is better than leaving a message that is incomprehensible and getting into a tangle so you have to ring off, or breaking into a fit of embarrassed giggles – this happened to a couple of students who wanted to call me once. I did not mind, but they said it was even more embarrassing to have to ring and record a second call.

BT at your service

All kinds of helpful business services are provided by British Telecom, and these are discussed under the appropriate headings in this book. For example conference calls under 'Meetings', fax (facsimile) under 'Correspondence', and so on. You will find it worthwhile to study the information pages of your district telephone directory and ring or write for extra data of any service you think your office might need some day, if not at once.

To sum up

To help you develop your telephone skills to a high level of competence, you should:

- Ensure you speak clearly (you can practise on a tape recorder)
- Treat the telephone as a person – be friendly when you reply
- Learn or devise a response that identifies your organisation
- Listen carefully to each caller's requirements
- Make notes during telephone calls (names, organisations, times)
- Check before putting callers through to other people
- Reassure waiting callers that you are trying to connect them
- Be tactful if calls are declined; try to help when you can
- If you take a message, check to see if the person responded
- Make notes of your needs before you make an outgoing phone call
- Be ready to use an answering machine to leave a clear message

4 Handling difficult people

- What do you do when people are unco-operative? contrary? or even aggressive?
- Can you keep your temper with unreasonable people?
- Is it true that a calm answer turns away wrath?

In any kind of office, you are liable to run up against difficult people. If you are really unlucky you could come across someone with whom – to quote the fashionable jargon – you have a 'personality clash' in your first weeks of a job. You might have been taken on to fill the post he or she hoped to be promoted into, for example. Or there could be someone on the staff who has built up a reputation for being difficult to deal with. 'Watch out for Mr Tanner; he'll make life hard for you if he can', or 'Ms Oakley has a low boiling point and she thinks that stationery cupboard is her private domain. Don't cross her or you'll have an argument every time you want a box of staples.'

Don't look for trouble

Naturally you should take these warnings to heart when you join a new office, but do not prepare for battle before you need to do so; Mr Tanner and Ms Oakley may have been given plenty of excuses for their aggressive attitudes by previous colleagues. They may be the kind of people who look to office life for a power base because they have no freedom outside work, such as heavy financial commitments that mean they are in a permanent anxiety state. By all means keep your head beneath the parapet but stay friendly and busy. It is quite hard to be unpleasant to someone who does not appear to notice barbed remarks because they are too preoccupied to hear them.

Quite often, the difficult people of office life get that way because colleagues treat them so cautiously. A newcomer may well be able to break the pattern by a courteous, confident approach.

'Will you say yes, or yes?'

With these types, giving them a choice of two decisions, both of which suit you, can be very effective. 'Ms Oakley, when I need more stationery, do you like to give it out item by item or is that too much of an interruption? Would you rather have a weekly list?' As for Mr Tanner, who was passed over for your job, he may respond if you show by your manner that you recognise his ability and experience. 'Mr Tanner, I've looked at the way these reports have been set out in the past and used the same sort of layout. Before I take this one through, could you just look at it and see if the style's right?'

You may well think that colleagues will see through these approaches but it is no bad thing if they do. At least they will appreciate that you are doing your best to fit in with the team, rather than demonstrating how knowledgeable you are.

Ditherers

At the other end of the personality spectrum are those people who fear and detest argument to the extent that they will do anything rather than give a definite opinion or supply information they may have to justify later.

They, too, are potentially difficult colleagues. They hesitate, dither and delay. Work gets held up because they will not make decisions on their own initiative. They are always waiting for someone else's authority to do anything from changing their lunch hour to ordering a motorbike courier. It can be maddening for a decisive person to be teamed with such an uncertain colleague and much patience is needed to arrive at a good working relationship.

Please tell me I am right

One of the things you can do is turn their pernickety nature into an advantage. 'Can you make one last check on this letter to make sure there are no mistakes? I think we can safely ring for a courier then.' Or, when they hesitate to respond to a client's request: 'Well, we certainly can't afford to upset this client, can we? As you say, he may already have had the full sales literature and price list. On the other hand, if I write a note on the compliments slip to the effect that I'm new and am sending it in case he hasn't seen it, people do make allowances for new staff. And it will show that we are doing our best to help whilst Miss Greenford is away. I could leave a note to say I've done it.'

Sharing the responsibility for someone's decisions should not deteriorate into doing their work for them. You may be responsible for training a junior. Once you are clear in your own mind about the work you want done and aware of how long it is likely to take someone inexperienced, you should leave them to get on with it. Stopping by the desk to say 'How are you getting on? Are there any problems?' is one thing. Checking up every half hour will only make the junior uncertain and is certainly likely to embarrass them in an office shared with other workers.

Pinpoint the problem

If you have someone working for you who seems hopelessly incompetent or unco-operative, you need to sit down and think why this might be. Is it because they have claimed skills at an interview that they do not possess?

Someone who badly wants a job may say that they can deal with reception, handle a switchboard and keep clerical records when in fact they hate dealing with phone calls and have a disastrous telephone manner. If the rest of their work is all right and you can pick out the fault, you may be able to correct it.

A spoonful of sugar

In a situation where you do not think someone is trying to be difficult but the effect is just the same – be tactful. Try to begin by saying something nice. For instance, 'It's nice to have someone so reliable keeping up the office diary and you're right, Bill, block capitals do make it much easier to get the names right. What I think we need to work on now is the right approach to phone calls. It would be more positive to say "Good morning – Smith, Jones & Green."' Try it. I think you will find people respond.

Sometimes a joke helps, 'Good heavens, John. Are you writing a novel? There's more paper on the top of this reception desk than in the files. You'd better clear it up; we can't even see the appointments book.'

Check on complaints

If you suspect that it is not inexperience or incompetence, but you are dealing with someone who is lazy, the first move is to check on what he or she does all day. Again, be pleasant about it. 'Jenny, I get the impression you're having a struggle to get through your work. Let's see if we can't sort out what has to be done and how long it should take. It may be that we need to reorganise who does what.'

That gives you a sound reason to check on how long Jenny is taking to sort and datestamp the mail, how much time she spends on the phone, and so on. Listen to excuses but check up on them. Jenny may be telling the truth when she says that every time she starts to deal with the paperwork, the phone interrupts her. If she has remembered to record all phone calls, she can prove it.

Working your way through problems

You may find someone has claimed skills they do not possess, or has been given work that is beyond them. There are various options for tackling this problem. If the person is very willing to learn, it is worth offering to teach them on the clear understanding that you are the one doing the favour if you come in early or stay late. If it is appropriate and you have the status to do it, you could offer to intercede with management to see if they can provide a training course and help with day-release or an early finish on the night the junior attends classes.

If you have made the mistake and taken on someone who has apparently claimed skills they do not possess, then you need to think carefully whether they are worth keeping. They may have displayed other abilities, such as the ability to get on with your clients, or work with the minimum of office equipment. (This is important in a small business where every penny counts.) On the other hand, you may have to suggest that they look for other work. It is particularly important in a small business that people should be compatible; you cannot 'carry' people who are not competent, either.

Trouble at the top

What about the difficult boss? There are many reasons why an executive can present as a 'difficult person'. He or she may be a delightful personality with a complete inability to refuse to help people, which means that impossible quantities of work mount up. In this situation, the first task must be to persuade the boss to prioritise – pick out things to be dealt with today and, if possible, this week (though this may be a herculean task at first). The 'softly-softly' approach is more likely to get results than forcing your efficient methods on an unwilling executive who will defend his or her territory and methods of working, however inefficient, when feeling threatened.

(Indecision is another exasperating trait in someone who has authority.)If your work depends on his or her decisions and they have to be dragged out of the individual concerned, the frustration of having to prod and persuade all the time is likely to send your blood pressure up until you yourself are in danger of becoming a difficult person. Bear in mind that the indecisive person is very often an uncertain one, so you will get much further if you can discover and/or establish precedents for action that must be taken. 'Mr Smith and Mrs Long tell me their departmental expenses go in on the last day of the month. You'll want me to send yours at the same time, I suppose?'

What me? difficult to work with?

Having considered difficult colleagues and difficult bosses, it is perhaps a good moment to consider whether *you* could possibly be regarded as a difficult person! Perhaps in a couple of years' time, with the benefit of hindsight, you may feel that in your early months at work, fresh from business college and full of bright new ideas that your office colleagues had never heard of, you must have been very exasperating.

If by the way people are treating you in the office you suspect that you appear to be a difficult person, listen carefully to what they say to you and consider how they treat you. Are you difficult because you are incompetent or careless? Those are problems you can rectify. Are you over-eager to please? There is a very delicate balance between showing you are keen to do well and pushing so hard for more work that you make people around you fear for their own jobs. You might have chosen the wrong environment, too. Not every office has a thrusting, competitive, commercial spirit. Not every office is a chatty, easy-going place. If by chance you have landed up in an environment that is all wrong for you, then do your best to match their needs. However, if after a few months you feel you will never fit in, it is best to move on. Having tried hard, you will probably go with a good reference.

Dear Sir! I must complain . . .

People outside the organisation can be difficult, too. They can write aggressive or threatening letters, be unhelpful or sarcastic on the telephone, even turn up to make a scene in the office. The full force of their anger is often directed towards the first person they meet, and that is not necessarily the person who really deserves it.

When you are faced with an aggressive person, it is natural to defend yourself. A positive reaction of this kind, though, is just what bullying types enjoy. If they can make you angry; if you let go of your self-control – why, you could well make a usefully damaging admission of guilt. You will probably be rude too; now there is another useful complaint they can make against you. Certainly you will not think clearly about the best way to deal with their complaint if you let yourself get agitated. In dealing with any type of difficult person, the first and golden rule is:

Don't lose *your* temper!

This sounds a very elementary piece of advice. Alas, it usually proves quite hard to follow. It is extraordinarily difficult to sit quietly whilst someone rants and raves in front of your desk. It is also upsetting to open a nasty letter of complaint when you have been sorting and date-stamping the rest of the post quite unsuspectingly. Even if you put it at the bottom of the pile, you know it is lurking there to wreck your day.

As for people who feel that they can be as rude as they like on the telephone, what a temptation it is to put the phone down and cut them off in mid-rant!

'Would you repeat that, please?'

One of the most disarming techniques when faced with a difficult person is to listen very attentively to his or her complaint. If you have the person in front of you, write down careful notes of what is said. With a telephone caller, interrupt politely to ask questions. 'Was that on the *10th* of January?', 'How do you spell your company name?; Is it B E E D Y Eye Detectives or is it B E *A* D Y?'; 'When were you expecting the parcel, Mr Caper?'

Demonstrating that you are taking notes does two things. If the aggressive person really does feel he or she has good reason to be so angry, then by making it clear that the complaint is being carefully recorded, you will help defuse the situation. You are demonstrating your concern at what has happened by recording exact details so that appropriate action can be taken.

On the other hand, if the aggressive person has simply flown off the handle at you as the nearest possible person to receive the anger, then asking them to repeat the allegations and checking facts so that the essence of the complaint is accurate will inevitably tend to slow down the whole process.

'Just to confirm the details . . .'

Do not let your angry complainant escape without reading back the notes you have taken. This is another technique that is both soothing and a protection for you and your organisation. Often enough, an enraged individual will want to see or talk to the management at once. On the other hand, when you have taken notes and the complainant knows you have taken them and checked them, he or she is far more likely to be willing to wait for a response.

Keeping your cool does not mean being icily polite; say what is going on and what you are going to do. Use the person's name – if they feel they have reason to be aggrieved, it is comforting to recognise that they have been taken seriously and their name has made an impression on the hearer. For example: 'Mr Caper. As I explained, Mrs Jones isn't in the office today, but I will pass these notes to her immediately she returns and we'll be in touch. I am sure she would want me to say we are concerned to have your complaint. We do have your phone number too, don't we? Caper Crisps, 0272 00272?'

To say that you are concerned does not commit your organisation to anything; it just shows attention to a client who has been upset.

'Your letter, received today . . .'

You can adopt the same approach for the person who has written an angry letter. He or she has been boiling over at the time it was composed and is probably imagining the upset that has been caused at the very moment you open the letter. An instant response will again soothe ruffled feathers. It confirms that the complaint has been taken seriously the moment it has arrived.

'I write to acknowledge . . .'

All you need to do is send a pleasant acknowledgement. You do not have to commit yourself or the organisation to regretting whatever has happened. It is quite enough to thank the client for their letter of (mention the date); to say you are concerned that they should feel there is reason for complaint and you will be in touch as soon as you have investigated the matter fully.

If you are answering on someone else's behalf, then adapt your letter slightly. You can still say that you feel the office manager will be concerned that there has been a complaint and that you will draw attention to the letter as soon as they return to work.

Dealing with scenes

Because the most urgent 'difficult people' to have to deal with are those who collect an audience around them (and that does nothing for the organisation's image), it helps to remove them from all those staring eyes. Be very polite. 'Mr Caper. I'm so sorry you feel like that. Please come through to the manager's private office at once.' With one deft action, you remove your complainant from the focus of attention and at the same time, demonstrate to the audience how concerned you are to deal with any dissatisfied individual. That turns a black mark into a bonus point.

Defuse the situation

Of course, some aggressive visitors will not obligingly move themselves away from their attentive audience. In that case, you have to take centre stage. 'Mr Caper,' you say, 'If you don't want to see any of our senior personnel, perhaps you'll explain the problem to me, now.' Then you should come out from behind your reception desk or enquiry counter or whatever the barrier is between you and the difficult person. This has the psychological effect of putting you both on the same side.

If it is possible for you to sit down beside the complaining person, this is again a non-aggressive action. By sitting, you show that the difficult person has nothing to fear from you. You are sitting down with all the time in the world (even if it is not true) to pay attention to what he or she has to say. It is ideal to have two seats side by side. If you are in a situation where you cannot sit down beside your client, make some believable excuse to come round from behind your counter. 'I'll just come round and look at that letter. Have you brought the envelope? It really does seem to have been very delayed.'

49

Record the facts

Again, do not forget your notebook and pen for recording details of the complaint. You are not just showing the dissatisfied client that you are concerned about the situation. You are also impressing the watching audience with your attention and courtesy to someone who in all probability is making an exhibition of himself or herself. Your good manners will be what people remember when they tell the tale later, 'This chap came in ranting and raving, and the receptionist was so patient; she came out and sat down to listen, made notes of what was wrong and promised to deal with it at once. You could see she really wanted to help.'

If in doubt, be kind

It never hurts to try and save someone's pride. Whether you are dealing with an aggressive client, an awkward colleague, an incompetent junior or a perfectly maddening boss, always begin by making allowances. You never know; the sullen man on the other side of the desk may have had a bereavement, be worried to death about the falling sales of his product or under pressure from his bank to pay off a loan. The bored teenager who spends half her time in the loo smoking instead of typing the invoices may not realise that they are not just a humdrum office routine to get through, but the source of the money that pays her. It is always better to jaw-jaw than war war as Winston Churchill advocated.

To sum up

When dealing with difficult people, it pays to:

- Listen to colleagues' warnings but make up your own mind
- Treat people as if you expect them to be pleasant
- Praise when you can, criticise when you must
- Look for reasons why people may be difficult or over-sensitive
- Make sure *you* are not provoking aggressive behaviour
- Record complaints, and read details to the person concerned
- Show concern for angry people; sit down to listen to them
- **Keep your temper** – it always takes two to quarrel

5 Dealing with correspondence

- What's the best way of dealing with incoming mail?
- How can you prove when a letter arrived?
- How do business letters differ from personal mail?
- How can you guarantee fast delivery of a letter?

Offices are our centres of communication. The importance of rapid and clear communication is underlined by the development of computers which can 'talk' to each other, and systems like telex and fax which convey information in the form of a print-out at the destination as fast as it is transmitted from the input point.

Keep it simple

Though it is important to be aware of this new technology, even in the most advanced of offices traditional correspondence still has to be handled. At the other end of the business scale, there are still many small companies without computers or word-processors. It is important to have a good system of handling correspondence that will work effectively with the minimum of equipment so that you can manage, if, for example, you are setting up your own business and want to keep costs down. But always be ready to learn new methods and take advantage of office systems that may make your work more effective.

Dealing with paperwork is something every office worker needs to be able to tackle efficiently, even though 'correspondence' today can include distributing computer print-outs or sending facsimiles (fax) as well as writing memos and letters and compiling reports.

Setting up a system – incoming mail

Few people need to be reminded that an outgoing letter should be dated, but it is just as important to date-stamp incoming communications. It can be very important to prove when a letter arrived in the office. Suppose a sought-after client writes for an urgent quotation, and his letter is delayed in the post? Someone with whom you have done a lot of business in the past might say 'That's unusual. Bussey & Co. usually reply by return' and would ring up to ask about the delay.

A new client, though, is just as likely to react by saying 'Well, they can't be very interested' and turn to another supplier. Then again, if someone has sent an invitation to a conference, or is applying for a job, or seeking views on a course of action that could affect your organisation, it could be important to be able to prove when the letters arrived. Failure to respond in time may be due to the inefficiency of a particular member of staff who finds it convenient at times to blame an apparent postal delay for any lack of response.

A further reason for date-stamping mail on the day of arrival may be that 'enquiries are dealt with in strict rotation'. This may be necessary when catalogues are being sent out in reply to an advertisement, or hospital appointments being made in response to doctors' requests. If someone rings up claiming that their letter has been ignored, it is valuable to be able to check back through the date-stamped mail and explain when it arrived, and when a reply can be expected.

'It arrived when?'

Sorting, date-stamping and distributing the post each day is often the responsibility of a comparatively inexperienced office worker who may be puzzled, for example, what to do about mail marked 'personal' or 'private and confidential'. There is usually an office regulation to say how you should treat these instructions. If such letters are to be passed to the addressee unopened, you can still date-stamp the envelope. The person concerned could be very grateful if the letter inside is dated as written several days ago. The delay may be nothing to do with the Post Office, but relate to an oversight in the sender's office. If the time of arrival is proven, the late response can be justified and the reason for delay investigated.

Date-stamping incoming mail can also be helpful when someone is away unexpectedly. You may be asked to take over and deal with anything that seems urgent, even if it is only to send a brief acknowledgement to people who appear to have been waiting for a response for several days.

It is very helpful to have a policy laid down as to what you should do about mail for someone who is away, and also if there is any kind of correspondence for which you have personal responsibility.

Speed + Care = Efficiency

For example, it may be your job to send out sales literature; an important one, for clients are impressed if their enquiry has a rapid response. You may be responsible for checking that clients ordering by post have actually enclosed the cheque or postal order they mention, and if they have not, sending a standard letter to point this out. Acknowledgements may be a routine policy – if a magazine offers a readers' advice service, they may send out an acknowledgement to say that the query has been passed to the appropriate expert and a reply can be expected in 4–6 weeks.

If you have not been given any regular task of this kind, but you can see from dealing with the incoming correspondence that there are matters you could deal with using a personalised standard letter, it is always worth suggesting the idea. Though you should be prepared for the idea to be turned down for a genuine reason, offering to take on an extra task of this kind marks you out as showing initiative and worth watching as you have the potential for more responsibility.

Read and learn . . .

Anyone who starts the day by opening, date-stamping and distributing mail has a marvellous opportunity to learn from the incoming correspondence. As you sort the letters, you can skim the contents. This not only lets you know about forthcoming events such as meetings, lunches or acceptances of interview dates that might need to be entered in the office diary but you can also learn about the problems the organisation may face, and about new projects in the pipeline or prospective clients who may ring (and be impressed if you recognise their name).

In planning your own office day, you can often get information from incoming mail that tells you to expect a session of dictation, or gives you advance warning that you may have to reorganise a meeting when someone important cannot make the proposed date. If you are given the privilege of access to incoming mail, it is common sense to learn from what you read.

Setting up a system – outgoing mail

In the same way, of course, you can learn from outgoing mail. In a small firm, it will help you to look through any outgoing correspondence, memos or reports that you are asked to dispatch in order to get an overall impression of the business and any developments that may be expected. If you work in one department of a large organisation, reading interdepartmental memos will help you understand how your department's work meshes with that of others, and keeping an eye on correspondence with clients will alert you to future projects, matters under discussion and so on. If your organisation is seeking new clients or building up business with existing ones, it is often worth making a note of the names of people who have been asked to 'get in touch' with regard to particular projects or quotations or meetings. They might phone instead of writing in response and, if you are aware of what is going on, you will know whether you should try to find the person who wrote the letter or gave the quotation; if you should take a message; or perhaps take notes and say you will ask the writer to ring back within 24 hours.

Rules of correspondence

If you are joining an established office, the first thing to do is to pay attention to the way letters are usually set out. Though you may feel it makes little difference to the clarity of a letter whether paragraphs are indented or not, or whether there are commas after each line of the typed address or not, employers usually like letters to be presented in a particular style. Look at the letter sent to you inviting you for interview offering you the job. This is likely to be in the 'house style'.

Even in the busiest office, you are not likely to be pitchforked into typing mounds of correspondence on your first morning, so take a look through any available file for evidence of preferred layout. The illustrations in this chapter suggest some common styles of correspondence. The address of the client may be heading the letter; following the letter and a typical layout used when the writer is on friendly terms with the addressee and likes to add a personal touch to business letters.

If you are someone setting up an office for your own business, it is worth bearing in mind that a style that does not involve the use of commas after each line of an address could be a good one to begin with.

If your business flourishes and you are able to buy a computer, you may want to use a 'mail-merge' system for personalising standard letters which depends on the computer inserting names and phrases separated by commas in a data file.

Time savers

For certain types of correspondence like invoices and statements, the use of window envelopes is valuable. By typing (or writing) the address at a certain level on the page, you can then fold your letter up so that the address shows clearly through the 'window' (the transparent panel) in the envelope. This may seem a trivial time saver, but if you have to type fifty letters a day, the time saved in typing fifty envelopes is considerable. Or if you write to some clients often, using pretyped sticky address labels is another time saver.

Keep it short

As far as content is concerned, the pitfall for most people is writing too much. Business schools will often tell you that if you need to go on to a second page when you are writing a letter, it is too long. It is true that if you try to make too many points in a letter, the really important ones will not be spotted.

There is no such thing as a blueprint for the perfect business letter. There are, however, guidelines you can follow if you find yourself in a situation where you have to compose a business letter on your own, or someone else's behalf.

Not too formal – not too slick

First, make sure you are writing to the right person and you have the right spelling for his or her name. (When in doubt, ring the other organisation's switchboard and check the spelling with their telephonist.) Old-style business letters would be addressed to John Smith Esq. (for Esquire) and you might begin 'Dear Sir' and end 'Yours faithfully'. You would only write to 'Dear Mr Smith' and end 'Yours sincerely' if you had actually met Mr Smith.

Today it is quite usual to use the 'Dear Mr Smith/Yours sincerely' formula if you have talked on the phone or had some sort of introduction to Mr Smith (perhaps you both attended the same meeting or work in the same office block). Or you may be writing to Mr Smith at the suggestion of his colleague, Mrs Jones. 'Yours truly' is a halfway house between 'Yours faithfully' (which goes with 'Dear Sir or Madam') and 'Yours sincerely' (which you can use with 'Dear Mr/Mrs/Ms/Miss Smith'). So you can use 'Yours truly' with either form of address.

Identify yourself

Unless you know the person you are writing to very well indeed, and sometimes even then (for instance, if your letter is likely to be shown to other people to whom you are not known) you would leave a space after 'Yours sincerely' for your signature and then type your own name (or write very clearly if the letter is handwritten). A married woman who likes using her title would put (Mrs) after her name. If you have a unisex name, like Chris or Alex for instance, the convention is to put (Mr) (Miss), (Mrs) or nowadays (Ms) may be preferred when you append your name to a letter. You may not mind too much if you are a woman and the person to whom you write replies to you as 'Mr Chris Jones', but it could be embarrassing for the writer to discover their mistake.

Another style of starting and finishing business letters to someone you know very well and have worked with for some time is to type his or her address in the usual way, but leave a space large enough to handwrite 'Dear Bill' or 'Dear Jill' and again at the end leave a space to handwrite 'Yours sincerely, Pat'.

Your letter will certainly need a date and if you are not going to be able to post until tomorrow, then tomorrow's date is more sensible than today's. It may also need a file reference number. Information systems vary a great deal between companies, but if it is an accounts matter, it might be INV/280/89 or if it is to do with personnel, a reference like PERS/YTS/DR may help the person sorting replies to make sure that the answer goes to the personnel department, and in that department, to the individual responsible for DR (Day Release) for YTS (Youth Training Scheme) participants. If you are starting up your own business you want a simple reference system that will make sifting your daily incoming post as easy as possible. Perhaps you have advertised your services in the *Herts Advertiser*, the *St Albans Review* and the *Daily Telegraph*, 'Please quote reference "HA" or "STAR," or "DT"' will be helpful in showing you which advertisement was most cost-effective.

Be precise but pleasant

What about content? 'Short and sweet' is what many people advocate, but even if you have only one question to ask, it can appear curt to write a one-sentence letter. I have seen examples of the 'Please attend for interview here on Thursday 12 January 1989' and 'Please let me know if you can give a 30-minute talk on "Telephone Technique" to the YTS trainees on the afternoon of January 5th or January 12th' variety. I find them off-putting and feel it is worth the few extra lines to say 'Thank you for your letter and application form' in the first instance, or 'You may know we operate a very successful Youth Training Scheme in this company. I would be very pleased if you would give a 30-minute talk on Telephone Techniques to the YTS participants. I suggest either Thursday January 5th or 12th and hope to hear that one of these dates will be suitable for you.'

If you are asking someone to come for an interview, attend a meeting or give a talk, it is sensible to ask them for a reply by a certain date. You could say 'Perhaps you would confirm that this time is convenient' in the case of the interview letter; or 'I look forward to hearing from you' in the case of the letter to the speaker on Telephone Techniques.

Capturing the reader's attention

In the beginning of this chapter, I discussed dealing with in-coming mail and suggested that the person responsible for distributing it could learn a lot by skimming through each letter. A quick skim through is all that a busy executive is likely to give any letter, so if you are writing on your own behalf as a self-employed person, it pays to use the first paragraph to capture the reader's attention by showing you have his or her needs in mind – not just yours. Some examples:

'I am writing at the request of your Sales Director, Linda Doze, who tells me you are looking for new designs for Dozy Duvet covers.'

'As promised when you visited our stand at the Conference Caterers' Exhibition, I enclose sachets of Bean and Bacon and Chicken and Ham Speciality Soups, together with the price list, though special rates may be appropriate in your case.'

'I see that the *Fast Foods Gazette* and *Quick Catering Review* carries a certain amount of advertising from caterers and I enclose a 300-word feature which I think might increase advertising potential as well as appealing to readers planning parties and weddings.'

Stating your business

The second paragraph of a business letter should state what you want, pleasantly but concisely. For Dozy Duvets, the writer might say 'I have around twenty new fabric designs to offer you and could visit your office with samples and my general portfolio for you to look through at a time to suit you. Six of my designs will be exhibited on the Colourways Art College stand at the Bedwear Show in March.'

For the letter to Speciality Soups, the second paragraph might say something like 'The views of your team on flavour and texture of these samples would be valued. If you can indicate the pack sizes most likely to be appropriate for your company, I can submit a quotation.'

In writing to the *Review* with a sample of work which the would-be freelance contributor hopes may interest the Editor and

Marketing Director, the second paragraph might read 'I hope to hear you are interested in this approach, and that we might talk over different ways of tackling the feature.'

Reasons for reply

The final paragraph of a letter of this kind can be designed to evoke a reply. For example, the Dozy Duvets letter might end 'Please let me know if you have an interest in any particular design so that I can bring a range of colourways.' The Speciality Soups letter might end with, 'We are able to quote for bulk soups to be repackaged under your own brand name. Please let me know if this is of interest when you reply.'

The letter to the *Review* might end, 'As is usual, I enclose a stamped addressed envelope for return of the sample article if you find it unsuitable in its present form. I can amend both style and length to suit your needs if this is required.'

The three samples I have outlined here are typical of letters that you might write to get a response. However, not every letter is designed to be answered. Sometimes a simple thank you for information or constructive criticism is required. Often a letter's purpose will be to convey information: 'Although we have retained our company name of Gammon, Hambone, Porkpie and Brawn, with effect from 1 January 1989 we will no longer produce potted brawn. We enclose details of our new range of country pâtés.' Or 'We are pleased to send you two tickets for the Conference Caterers Exhibition, where Speciality Soups will be exhibiting on Stand 101 and look forward to meeting old and new customers.'

Brief notes

Often a brief note, memo or typewritten reminder on a compliments slip is enough to give information without bothering with a letter. A clinic appointment may be sent with an attached note: 'You are advised that when attending the eye clinic, certain procedures can be lengthy and it is suggested that you come prepared for the delay, which sometimes is inevitable.' (That is a note from a real hospital, by the way, though I added two commas.)

Stand-ins

Everyone takes holidays and most of us are unlucky enough to fall sick at some time during our working lives, so there needs to be a system for dealing with any individual's correspondence during an absence. If you are a newcomer to an organisation, there is likely to be someone you can turn to for advice; one of the executives or perhaps someone working at the same level of responsibility as your own, but in another department.

Actual decisions on how to deal with problems or requests that may turn up in the mail for someone who is away may be taken by a more senior staff member but quite often it will be your job to explain them. As with telephone calls, nothing is more annoying for a client to be left 'hanging on' and wondering if he or she will ever get a reply, so the first rule is to acknowledge that letter has been received, though the addressee is away.

A choice of action

You may then be able to give the writer a choice of two options. Say something like 'Due to illness, Mrs Clancy is not likely to return to the office until early February. Perhaps you would let me know if you want her to contact you then, or if her deputy, Mr Peter Marks, could be of assistance. He is dealing with all urgent matters during Mrs Clancy's absence.'

What if you are self-employed and you are ill? It does happen, and though you may have a relative or friend who will help out as much as possible (you certainly *should* organise something of the sort in advance when starting up a business on your own account), you do need to make it easy for them. Just as you can put a message on a telephone answering machine, so you can devise standard letters that your stand-in can photocopy as required, filling in the appropriate address and the date, and send off on your behalf, to cover any temporary difficulty.

You might want to say something like this, 'Thank you for your enquiry. At present, I am not able to take on extra work/new commissions/quote for repairs but I am grateful for your interest and will be in touch as soon as possible.' You may feel that it is appropriate for your kind of business to have a second version of this short letter, which adds a paragraph saying, 'It is always encouraging to be approached by potential clients and I hope to have another chance to quote for your requirements in the future.'

The tactful option

You will notice that I have not mentioned illness or holiday as an excuse for being unable to deal with the enquiry. This is always a matter for personal judgement. If you are working for a giant organisation like ICI or the BBC or British Aerospace, it is usually quite acceptable to say that someone's away sick or on holiday. But with a very small business, clients can react oddly in these circumstances. There is a certain attitude of mind that says 'small may be beautiful, but large is safe'; in other words in a one-man-band or a partnership, you could be taking a bit of a chance in employing them. It is often better not to say you are turning away work because you are sick or on holiday (it implies that everything stops when you do, which may be true, but is not a very good advertisement). You do not have to lie and say that you cannot take on the work because you are already committed but, at the same time, there is no reason to even give a hint that you might be unable to work because you are not well, or because you cannot afford a stand-in.

Use the cost of postage

Small firms need to make use of every opportunity to get information across for the cost of a stamp. If a customer orders a booklet, you can enclose a list of other publications when you send it. If you are running a club of any kind, a neatly typed or printed enclosure when you acknowledge subscriptions, send out the newsletter or post off tickets that have been paid for can list all the additional services the club provides (with appropriate fees) and be used to recruit new members. It is quite usual to find a little note inside a subscription reminder saying something like 'If you'd like us to send details of membership to a non-member friend, please write the name and address below and return to the club at the address above. We'll do the rest!' If you run a cattery and are sending out bills, you can tuck a memo with your 1989/90 opening and closing dates in the same envelope. Postage can be an important cost in the operation of any business.

Second class, first class, data post, fax . . .

It sounds like a playground rhyme – you could certainly skip to it – which is what you could also find yourself doing if you absent-mindedly send out a vital quotation by second class mail, or inadvertently used first class stamps to send out hundreds of leaflets which are not urgent. Understanding the rules for mailing correspondence in your organisation is a vital part of effective office management, and it is certainly something that should go in the Office Notebook, referred to often in this book.

You will probably find that your office keeps a copy of the *Post Office handbook* and the British Telecom *Products and services* supplement for reference. They may also keep a range of leaflets from independent courier and delivery services; you have probably heard of people like TNT and City Link and Red Star, but the local *Yellow Pages* directory will alert you to many more.

For your Office Notebook

If you join an established company, not only are you likely to find an agreed policy for dealing with mail, and a system whereby you can frank your own correspondence, or keep a stock of stamps of different values in the office, but you will probably deal with specific companies. Your organisation may prefer a specific courier service, or always ask you to call a particular cab company for delivering large items (say a large piece of artwork between the design agency that produced it and the advertising agency for whom it is intended). Take note of these systems; quite often they denote that as a regular customer, your employing organisation may have negotiated special rates.

Everyone, though, needs to understand the Post Office, British Telecom and British Rail systems of communication because they are so widely available. You need to be able to decide between Recorded delivery and Registered post; consider whether to send a Telemessage, a Telex or a Fax or whether you should use a 'same day', 'overnight – delivery by 9 a.m.' or 'delivery next day' service. Some companies have radio-controlled motorcycle and courier vans which they can call up to arrange collection and subsequent delivery of very urgent items.

Technology speeds things up

Most business college leavers have been taught about the use of telex and fax (facsimile) services. People returning to an office environment after a long break, and newcomers to office routine, like the person starting up in business may not fully understand them. Telex is an electronic system which can send words and figures from a machine in your office (or offered as a service by a local office bureau) so that they appear on a machine in the recipient's office. Fax is an electronic system which can transmit whole documents including pictures or diagrams as well as words and figures across the miles. Both systems involve the use of a telephone to call up the special telex or fax number to which you want to send a message.

Your local telephone directory should contain advertisements both for postal service information, with numbers to ring for details of special business services; for British Rail and for British Telecom. The latter has a very good free supplement describing 'Products and services'. Keep your office's stock of these national information leaflets, and leaflets from other delivery and courier services up to date.

Keep an eye on costs

Do not forget also to update price lists regularly. Postage costs usually depend on weight (you will need an office weighing machine or to find out the least busy time of day to use the local post office machine). Express delivery services relate not only to the distance covered, but the speed of delivery required (same day, overnight with arrival by 9 a.m. or overnight with arrival by noon). As far as fax services are concerned, there can be considerable cost differences between bureaux. Usually there is a high charge for the first item transmitted, reducing for subsequent pages.

It follows that you need to know the telex or fax number of the organisation you want to contact. Sending a telex or fax may imply that you possess one, so, to save the recipient spending time fruitlessly trying to find a number through which they can send a return 'electronic message', it is as well to add a line to your message. Something like 'Sent via fax bureau; please reply by phone or letter' could save a lot of frustration.

Electronic mail box

As this is a book about running your office rather than managing your computer, it is not the right place to search for details of the most advanced communication systems of the electronic office. But we all know, from TV advertisements if not from direct experience, that there are systems available whereby computers can be connected by a unit called a 'modem' which makes it possible to type a letter or enter a set of statistics on one computer and then transmit this material so that it appears on the visual display unit of another computer by using a special telephone connection and keying in the material by following instructions which appear on your own computer's screen.

Incidentally, this kind of electronic mailing system does not just apply between computers in the same office or the same building; it can operate between cities too.

Inter-office memos

It can come as quite a surprise to discover that you have to put as much effort into what you say in a memo to be sent to all staff or displayed on internal notice boards as you do when you are writing letters to outsiders. But whereas in a letter, though you should not ramble on, you do have space to explain yourself, the brevity of a memo can easily make it seem curt. Colleagues are people, just like the organisation's clients, and you need to grab their attention with a heading if you want your memo to be read or noticed by the passing crowd if it is designed for the departmental notice board.

Eyecatchers

In an ideal world, office notice boards would not be covered in overlapping dog-eared notices referring to events long since over. Bearing in mind that they usually are, you must devise a relevant and eye-catching heading for your memo: OFFICE TOILETS TO CLOSE! should certainly alert everyone to the fact that the plumbers will be working between 2 p.m. and 4 p.m. on Friday afternoon. If you are seeking more recruits to a lunch-time training session, FREE! always catches the eye. Then, on the second line, you can put WORD-

PROCESSOR TRAINING, Wednesday & Thursday lunch hours. Book with Mr P. J. Smith, extension 44.

WARNING! is another key word. Send round a memo explaining that in an effort to reduce the number and duration of telephone calls, each telephone will be monitored and the calls charged to the budget of the department concerned and you will find people tend to stop reading after the first line. Head it WARNING! PHONE CALLS TO BE MONITORED and everyone who uses the phone will scan the small print that follows to ensure that Big Brother is not checking to see who makes personal calls in the firm's time.

You will have recognised in reading through this chapter that the essence of being a good correspondent is to *communicate*.

To sum up

Handling correspondence effectively on your own and others' behalf depends on having efficient systems for:

- Recording and monitoring incoming mail
- Agreeing a policy on dealing with mail for absent colleagues
- Adopting an agreed style of layout for letters and memos
- Taking care to spell names and get job titles correctly
- Writing pleasant, concise letters that attract replies
- Acknowledging incoming queries if answers may be delayed
- Keeping up to date with postal, courier and rail delivery services
- Choosing the right system for each item of correspondence
- Learning to use the new electronic communication systems

NB *Most office managers would agree that the most important factors in dealing efficiently with correspondence are to know exactly when a communication arrived and the quickest way to get a reply back to the sender. If yours is a new small business and you cannot afford elaborate equipment, you can meet both needs by buying and using an inexpensive date stamp and finding out about local firms' telex, fax, overnight delivery and courier services.*

6 Filing – information flow and retrieval

- Why should a filing system be simple?
- What does cross-referencing mean?
- How do you use an index system?
- Should you rely on computers?
- Where can you get advice on information sources?

The trouble with filing systems is that you have to know where to look for the information hidden in them. This is equally true whether you have the latest computer set-up or are trying to cope with a set of labelled cardboard boxes.

The single most important factor in dealing with information is to make it possible for *anyone* to use the system. That means putting in information under as many categories as might be needed to make the data accessible to someone with very little knowledge of the organisation as well as to someone with specialised knowledge who has been there for years. It also means cross-referencing the entries, so that if a complete newcomer picks his way through the alphabetical index looking for clues to the data needed, there will be a directory of places in which to find it.

If in doubt, be obvious

If you are just starting off in business and are at the cardboard box on the kitchen unit stage, you may be comforted to know that in the electronic office of some high-powered supplier, an inexperienced office worker could well be staring at a computer VDU screen desperately trying to remember where they might have filed *your* details. Let's imagine that you have called your business 'Anniversary Caterers' and your special gimmick is that you pride yourself on giving a rapid service for last-minute parties, elopements, or celebrations. Because you have had no answer to your detailed enquiry about Speciality Soups, you have phoned for information – but the Sales Manager is in difficulties, because his data clerk cannot find your original letter.

67

Where would *anybody* look?

So far, your enquiry does not seem to be filed under *Caterers –
Freelance* or *Caterers – Local* or *Caterers – Wedding*, any one of which
sounds a likely possibility. Maybe it is under the name of your firm. Now
what was it again?

Alas, the alphabetical index does not include Anniversary Catering and it is no good the Sales Manager hopping from foot to foot,
hissing anxiously, with his hand over the mouthpiece of the phone, 'You
must remember them. They were the instant people. I remember them.
They wrote in saying they could cater for ten at a moment's notice, fifty
at a morning's notice, a hundred at a day's notice. Where is their
enquiry?'

But under *I* for *Instant* there seem to be only couriers and dry
cleaners. *E* for *Emergency* just has doctors and dentists.

Ages later, your data turns up. The data clerk explains that it was
filed under *J* for *James*. *J* for *James*? Crazy as it sounds, there was a
certain purpose to her system when she explains it:

'Well, Bill James is Speciality Soups salesman for Berkshire – so
when Anniversary Caterers enquired about instant soup sachets in
catering packs, they were entered under *R* for *Representatives*, sub-file *S*
for *Southern area* and alphabetically under *J* for *James*. That meant they
would automatically be included in his print-out of potential clients to
visit. My print-outs are sent to each representative on Thursday so they
arrive in time for the next week's calls to be planned. So I filed Anniversary Caterers where they'd automatically appear on Mr James' list.'

This is an example of how a filing system can go wrong when it is
operated from the point of view of a single individual. It can be a very
common fault to let the information store be the private fiefdom of
someone who specialises in operating it and jealously guards his or her
system – like that particular data clerk.

'Of course, if Anniversary Caterers had been an *actual* client
rather than a *potential* client, they would certainly have been entered
under *C* for *Caterers* and put in the alphabetical index. But they are not
yet clients, only possibilities. That's why I put them in the *Representatives*
file', she explains helpfully.

At this point, the average Sales Manager is likely to explode and
proceed to make it very plain that whether actual or potential clients, and

whether they are *Caterers, Colleges, Circuses* or *Choir schools*, any organisation likely to buy Speciality Soups should be filed where anyone in the firm can find them if they ring up!

Here, there and everywhere

This is an exaggerated example to illustrate the value of cross-referencing (which has nothing to do with angry managers). Cross-referencing means you can make an entry in more than one file when you are dealing with data that people might need to find for different purposes. You can cross-reference a short entry to direct the enquirer to a more detailed one.

The trick is to think up all the possible categories in which someone might think of filing and then make sure their name is listed under every one of these headings. It only needs to be a mention; the detailed explanation can be kept to one section, to which you are referred across – that is, it is 'cross-referenced'.

You do not have to be the custodian of a computer to find this a useful system. Taking as an example, the data clerk was right to enter Anniversary Caterers under *Representatives* (James – Bill). Indeed, the company's policy of recording names and addresses of possible new customers in this way and regularly printing them off to send to their sales representatives, is a very practical use of stored information. This kind of use is often built into the system using the information store as a 'time reminder'. You have seen how it can work to have a data file, which once a week is printed off and sent out to all the company representatives.

Tagging for regular recall

A different kind of use for stored information might be used by a hospital to recall patients who need regular blood tests, for example. Each time such a patient's file is withdrawn, it can be electronically tagged if it is a computer system, or with a colour code if it is a manual one, so as to denote when that patient should get a recall notice. With the computer, you can instruct it to hunt through its list of patients for any names tagged with a date. With a manual system, you can look through your card index for any which display an orange label on which the recall date is listed. Remember to explain any identification system of this kind in your Office Notebook and cross-refer to the office year planner if you use one, so that anyone who might be standing in for you when you are away will have his or her attention drawn to the fact that the filing system incorporates a time-reminder scheme.

Starting points

This is an example of using an information system to help you deal with a regular assignment. You can also enter information in such a way so that it is discovered without effort when an unexpected need crops up.

Going back to Anniversary Caterers, as well as being listed alphabetically in the card index, the filing system could include this firm under *Caterers – Local, Caterers – Freelance* and indeed, in both the *Instant* and *Emergency* files.

Suppose Speciality Soups had to set up an urgent press conference to deal with the suspicion that their product might have been involved in an outbreak of food poisoning at a local hotel. Although Anniversary Caterers are potential *customers* for their products, being reminded that they are on the doorstep (because they are listed under *Instant* or *Emergency* or *Caterers – Local*) could mean they also have potential as *suppliers* of a service needed by Speciality Soups.

Attracting attention

In this situation, what matters most is making it easy for the user of an information store to come across the data that is needed. Within reason, the more cross-references you can make, the more useful your information store is likely to be. Only the major entry needs to give full details of the organisation. The subsidiary just mentions the name and directs the information-seeker to the main, detailed entry.

For Anniversary Caterers, common sense suggests the main entry should be under *Caterers* as that is the business concerned. And since it could be convenient to call on a nearby caterer, the place where Anniversary Caterers should have its main entry would probably be in *Caterers – Local.*

At the same time, there are reasons for cross-referencing to this main entry from other files. Where these brief entries are concerned, all the data clerk need enter in the way of information is 'Anniversary Caterers, see *Caterers – Local*'.

Checking up

The 'local' aspect could be very useful if Speciality Soups public relations officer rings up asking if there are any nearby customers who might be willing to give their views of the product to a television crew following up the food poisoning story.

Or, on a happier occasion, and remembering the possibility of cross-referencing them under *Caterers – Freelance*, the advertising department might seek a list of small specialised caterers to put in an advertisement on the lines of 'From Ancient to Modern, Speciality Equals Quality', picturing different users of the product; from a traditionally-uniformed waitress placing a soup tureen on the dining table of an historic Cambridge college to you loading your Anniversary Caterers van with packs of Speciality Soup, followed by someone carrying a wedding cake.

If you have the latest electronic information system, then locating data you need may simply involve typing in the title or reference of a data file, which results in the information flashing onto a computer screen in seconds.

Retracing helpful people

But even if you store your files in a cardboard box, you can still use cross-referencing to speed things up. You can make your own card index by cutting up sheets of card and separating them with larger, thicker cards.

Each of the separating cards needs a stand-up letter of the alphabet. You can then give each of your clients, suppliers, or officials you have to deal with a separate card. On this you can put their personal details, plus any important cross-references.

Taking a Tax Office contact as an example, the person may be called Chris Bramley. Being able to trace him could be important if you open your post one day and discover an unexpected demand for some horrifying estimated amount of a tax you had not realised you might be eligible to pay.

You probably have a file or folder for all the letters, photocopied forms and booklets you have to deal with for tax purposes. But before you rush to sift through that and start worrying because you cannot read the signature of the person who wrote the last letter, turn to your card index.

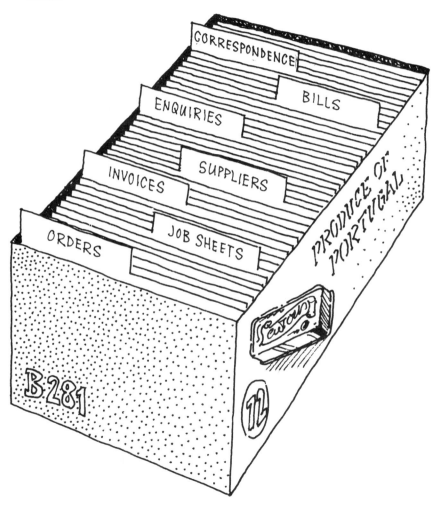

Old contacts can solve new problems

You should have a card for *Tax* under *T*. With good planning, it should refer you to your *Contacts* file under *C* saying something like 'recent contact, Chris Bramley, see *Contacts*'.

If you have kept your index up to date, then working your way alphabetically through the *Contacts*, you should come across *Bramley (Mr Chris)*. The Mr is important as Chris is a name that could apply to a man or a woman and it is easy to forget individuals you have talked to on the phone if many months have elapsed between calls. On Mr Bramley's card, you should have his job title (is he an Executive Officer, a Higher Tax Officer, or a Tax Adviser?); when you last had dealings with him and why; his phone number and his extension.

You can see that this could be very helpful to you in dealing with the tax letter that has thrown you into a panic. Even if Chris Bramley himself is not in when you phone, the fact that you know his extension means you are through to the right office; you will not spend ages with the switchboard operator trying to find out who should be dealing with an enquiry about allowable expenses for some aspect of catering. Being able to refer to an employee, whether it is the Tax Office or another business, implies that you have had friendly dealings with them before – another plus factor. And if you do get through to Chris Bramley it helps that you remember him as another person, not just a faceless official who sent you a form.

Obviously just getting hold of the relevant file will not necessarily solve your problem. You will also need to have your *Tax* file with all the recent correspondence in it so that you can refer to dates and reference numbers. One without the other will not be very helpful. The value of cross-referencing *Bramley (Mr Chris)* both under *Contacts* and under *Tax* could be equally valuable if you get a sudden phone call from a chap who says 'Anniversary Caterers? My name's Chris Bramley, like the apples, and we were in touch in May last year.' As you are frantically trying to remember why you should have spoken to a man called Bramley last May, you can be checking through the *B*s entered in the *Contacts* section of your card index to track him down. If you need to buy time, remember you can always say 'Oh, Mr Bramley, please excuse me a moment while I finish my other call,' and use both hands to sift through the card index!

Old technology has its uses

Even with a computer, or perhaps particularly with a computer, it is useful to have a card index on your desk that shows you where different categories of information are kept.

Computer systems let you set up your own electronic index, but sometimes it could be quicker to check through a card index or leaf through a list of disc reference numbers in order to get the information you need rather than have to take discs in and out of a computer and hunt through different electronic indices for it.

Classify and clarify

Some files, whether manual or electronic, need to contain so much information that they are unwieldy to use. Storing important data may involve keeping hundreds of pages up to date. To use the data efficiently, it needs to be broken down into convenient chunks, with each section given an identifying label.

An example? Well I have worked with a computer system that stores information on different careers. They are indexed in various ways, the first being the use of reference numbers approved by the national public library and careers service system for filing career facts.

A typical index system

This is called the 'Careers Library Classification Index' and it lists related careers under a letter classification applied to all jobs in that occupational area. '*L*' means Law; but *LAB* covers information about Barristers; *LAC*, Solicitors; *LAD*, Legal Executives, and so on.

Useful though this is, there could be several entries needed for any one career, e.g. *LAC – Solicitor* might have to contain information on entry requirements, methods of training, job content, employers with training places, professional associations and sources of training. People looking for information on training to be a solicitor might want to know the names of universities and polytechnics where they can take a law degree or a preliminary course in law or a correspondence course.

Reviewing all this material that is likely to be needed or at least useful in the *LAC – Law careers* field, you can see it could take ages to read or scroll through on a computer if it is simply entered in one long chapter of information. *LAC*, therefore, could do with a subsidiary reference system to make it quick to use. Let's consider how this could be devised.

Breaking down the information

Perhaps *LAC–1* could be used for entry requirements and *LAC–2* might cover methods of training; *LAC–3* might cover job content; *LAC–4* list employers with training places and *LAC–5* preliminary courses. *LAC–6* could list degrees; *LAC–7* professional qualification courses and *LAC–8* correspondence courses. *LAC–9* could be used to identify professional associations.

LAC–2 – methods of training could be usefully cross-referenced to *LAC–5*, *LAC–6*, *LAC–7* and *LAC–8*.

Therefore, someone who wanted information on methods of training using a correspondence course could be sent a print-out of *LAC–2* and *LAC–8* plus *LAC–9* in case they wanted further specialised professional information.

Though this is the sort of system that could work very well with a computerised information store, it could also be used with information stored on paper and photocopied. It does not matter whether *LAC–8* identifies electronic data on correspondence courses in law, or the same material on a printed sheet taken from a conventional filing cabinet.

Simplifying indices

You might think that specialised classification indices are easy enough to use. Have you not just discovered that using the official Careers Library Classification Index identifies Law with the letter *L*? Alas it does not go on that way. For instance, in that particular index, Health & Medical Services are identified with the letter *J* which may mean that it is easy to remember data on medicine is stored under *JAB*!

But would you have thought of *JAM* for orthoptics, or *JOG* for medical illustration? Most of us would not, which is why it is necessary to have a simple alpabetical index with items cross-referenced under all the different headings one might think of.

Systems explained

I have used samples from the Careers Library Classification Index because I am familiar with it, but there are many other specialised systems for identifying data stores. Your public library almost certainly uses the Dewey Classification System which again combines letters and numbers.

Even so, to make it easy for everyone to use the library and find the books they need, there are catalogues, both fiction and non-fiction, listing books by both author and title. If you know the name of either, the catalogue will give you the Dewey identification so you can go straight to the shelf containing books labelled with those particular letters and numbers.

Office filing systems are organised in a similar way. When a firm is starting up, it is probably quite adequate to use an index and a box or drawer or files. Only when the information coming in begins to get more complicated are you likely to need a system like the one I illustrated for storing careers information about becoming a solicitor.

If you go to work for a long-established organisation, you will probably be expected to learn how to use their particular filing system, which should make storing and retrieving their specialised information as easy as possible.

Keeping people out

Some kinds of information need to be kept confidential. Examples are government or military intelligence, medical records, or company personnel department information about private matters. You would not want to make this so accessible that anyone passing through the office can ferret through it at will.

Quite often it is necessary to put up confidentiality barriers on information stores. Nowadays, computers can have special codes built in to prevent people reaching sensitive information, and only eligible individuals are trusted with the formula to bring up 'Code yellow' or 'Code purple' which would be a security barrier. With manual systems, confidential information may be kept in locked cabinets to which only 'designated' staff have the keys.

Data Protection Act

It is strange but true that if I choose to keep details of everyone I interview in an alphabetical card index left on my desk (which presumably any inquisitive soul could flip through) I am free to do so, and there is also no rule to prevent me storing detailed files of information in a manual system, such as a set of filing cabinets or an open filing tray.

However, if I should put the same sort of information on a computer (which most people need special training to operate), I would be in trouble unless I had registered with the Data Protection Register. Since November 1987 we all have a right to see data held about us in a computer file from which we can be identified. Knowing how to register could be important for someone setting up a small business and keeping files of information on clients and potential clients. *Data protection: Putting the record straight* by Roger Cornwell and Marie Staunton (National Council for Civil Liberties 1985) sets out how you should register if you are going to store this data.

Good data housekeeping

There can be few of us who have not written off for some product or service at some time and had our letter returned, marked 'Gone away'. Similarly with office files, you have to be on the lookout for changes of address and changes of personnel, so that you can update your files. People, in fact, are more likely to go out of date than addresses.

Quite often I have to write to a range of higher education colleges seeking information on courses. Though I keep a 'contacts' book, like most journalists, with names, jobs and phone numbers of knowledgeable and helpful people, it is a sad mess of crossings-out and new entries. Perhaps people working in colleges move jobs very frequently, but certainly on occasions when I have used official 'Information Officer' lists produced by academic organisations, there are always four or five brochures which come complete with a compliments slip saying things like: 'Angus Smith has left. I am now Information Officer – Susan Scraggs.' Next time around I may well be told that Susan Scraggs has been appointed to the Registrar's office and Jim Hurtle now runs the Information Service. When possible, I change these entries in my contacts book as soon as they are notified because I am likely to have to ring individuals for urgent information.

Update regularly

The other vital task, that of regularly going through your files to remove inaccurate or out-dated material is a bit like spring cleaning your paperwork. You have to plan to do it at the least busy time of year; if you are not the decision-maker in your office but the custodian of the filing system, then you have to time your data spring clean for the time when the person in charge can give you the OK to consign old files to the basement or put letters through the shredder.

Don't be a data hoarder!

Overflowing folders, great toppling masses of leaflets that might be useful some day and/or sets of computer discs that react to the insertion of new material with the message 'DISC FULL – AM DELETING OLD .BAK FILE TO MAKE SPACE' are no aid to efficiency. Making your information easily accessible often means getting rid of anything you do not really need to store.

That includes anything that is more convenient to access in books: why copy out pages of addresses if you can refer enquirers to a reference book, specialised library or a specialised computer index, such as *PRESTEL*? The latter is the British Telecom information service and it is worth getting details of this, or of any specialised information service that relates to the kind of business you are in. To give you an example, there is a data base of further and higher education courses and their entry requirements known as *ECCTIS* (Educational Counselling and Credit Transfer Service) to which careers information staff can sub-scribe. Many different kinds of businesses have their own computerised data bases relating to the sort of subjects that concern them. Pro-fessional institutes and trade organisations can advise on this.

Go to the experts

There are also libraries which supply information for people with particular interests. I once researched an enquiry about the possible use of caffeine in the treatment of epilepsy, starting out at my public library, being referred on to *ASLIB* (the Association of Special Libraries and Information Bureaux), from them to a national scientific library, then to a specialised library of world medicine, and finally ending up with reports of a clinical trial held at a hospital in Switzerland. If you are ever asked for a piece of information and you cannot think where to find it, always begin by seeking the advice of the librarian in your local public library. Librarians are experts on classification systems, so if you find yourself getting bogged down with tags and terminals, seek help from the nearest public library. They will know exactly how to tackle the problem.

To sum up

The purpose of having an office filing system is to store information that is useful, accurate and easily found. Managing it efficiently demands that you:

- Enter data under obvious headings for the average user
- Cross-reference entries to cater for special information needs
- Use an index as a quick-reference guide to the system
- Break down information into easily-found segments
- Make extra use of a data base by inserting time reminders
- Keep your files up to date; weed out unnecessary data
- Build in confidentiality safeguards where needed
- Make sure you satisfy any Data Protection Register needs
- Extend your data sources with library and computer data bases and above all . . .

Explain your filing system to other users

7 Briefing and debriefing Representing the organisation

- How do you represent someone else?
- What are the priorities when briefing a stand-in?
- What are the pitfalls in a new situation?
- How do you extract a full report after the event?

We all know what a briefing is. Anyone who has seen a World War II flying film knows that it is when all the pilots file into the hangar and the group captain strides on to the platform and says 'Quiet now, chaps' as the lights are dimmed and the map is revealed behind him. Then with a pointer, he indicates the targets for his group, how they are to be reached, when they are to be struck and why this is all so important.

There is not a lot of difference between this scenario and the average business briefing. The surroundings may be more luxurious, the group captain less impressive as a civilian and the map replaced by a list of customers or the catalogue for an exhibition. But the fundamental theme will be the same. Your task in representing the organisation is to get amongst the competition and target on this or that objective, without ever forgetting why you have been sent and in whose name.

Why you?

People may represent their department or firm at exhibitions, press conferences, sales meetings and demonstrations. They may be sent along just as a presence, to make sure that the organisation is recorded as having been represented. Or they may have specific instructions to achieve something – make a contact or obtain certain information. Quite often they are sent as researchers, not because they have the authority to order new office furniture or a full-colour photocopier, but because having to use the equipment day in and day out has made them the ranking expert.

Anyone who sees this experience as a jolly day out of the office will probably not get the chance to tackle it more than once. Choosing someone to represent the organisation is not something any manager regards lightly. You are there as the face of the firm and because it is felt you will represent the organisation's ideas and objectives efficiently. Be sure that any calamitous mistake you make, whether babbling about the company's sales plans to a competitor, or drinking rather too much of the free wine, will get back to the management. Equally, if you lurk unobtrusively in a corner, physically present but mentally absenting yourself from the discussions and events that are going on, you will have a job explaining why it was worth sending you when you finally return to the organisation.

What are you doing there?

A lot of the failings of those sent off to represent their organisations on behalf of people too busy to attend themselves are due to inadequate briefing. 'Oh dear, oh dear,' says the overworked executive. 'Two conferences on the same day and I ought to go to both of them. Well, Perks, I must go to the merger meeting. You will just have to represent me at the Fast Foods Fair and for goodness sake, look respectable and don't miss any of the stands that might be relevant to our business.'

Poor old Perks. If this represents the limit of his briefing before the Fast Foods Fair, all kinds of traps await him at what he probably sees as a pleasant break from routine; wandering round the exhibition and nibbling at the free food samples.

Pitfalls for the unwary

One is the 'poor old feet' trap. Tramping around exhibitions in your best clothes, which also often means your newest, tightest shoes, you are a natural target for the exhibitor who has something to gain from you. 'Come in, sit down and have a drink,' says this affable soul. 'Gosh, these places get hot, don't they? Let's see, where are you from? Oh, Gammon & Co. Good firm. Pity about the merger, though.'

If the visitor is not very careful, he will respond, as intended, with 'Oh, nothing's been agreed about the merger yet. I'm here today because the top brass are all at a meeting with Pressed Pork Products to see if it's feasible.' Just what the competition wanted to know so that they could rush round both Gammon, Hambone, Porkpie and Brawn and Pressed Pork Products' customers with the hot news of a probable merger. 'And you know what that means. They'll cut back on the product range; always happens when people decide to rationalise production. Now our company will be widening its range of products in 1989 . . .'

Don't enjoy yourself too much!

Then there is the demon drink problem. At exhibitions, presentations, and even inter-office Christmas parties, beware of those bearing brimming glasses of wine, punch or other alcoholic brews. The time to let your hair down is in your own time, not on company time. If you are a shy person, not a party-goer, who is only at the event because it has been presented as one of your work responsibilities, you are an easy target for the hospitable, chatty type who keeps topping up everyone's glass.

This may sound as if every business get-together is a boozy battleground, but in practice, refreshments (which include alcoholic drinks) are provided at most all-day events. Even if a competitor does not set out to be sneaky and pick up snippets of information about your organisation that would be useful for his or her own, drink does loosen the tongue and relax the inhibitions. You can let out background information about your company without intending to do so or even being provoked into demonstrating your knowledge.

Suppose you are at an office equipment exhibition, looking at photocopiers. Chatting over your company's needs for an extra photocopier because of the queues to use the present one, you may impress the salesman that any photocopier that may be offered must be able to reproduce colour copies because you are 99% certain of getting lots of short-run print orders for Anniversary Caterers, who like to provide clients with illustrated menu cards as souvenirs for guests to take away. Because you are slightly merry, it does not cross your mind to look round and see who might be listening as you voice your requirements.

Beware of eavesdroppers

Oops! You have just dropped two valuable pieces of information into the listening ear of the alert visitor from Cheeryprint Copies. He now knows that Anniversary Caterers are in the market for a good deal on short-run colour photocopies. And then he realises that he can go to the other caterers and say, 'You know, of course, that Anniversary Caterers make a feature of providing illustrated guest menus as souvenirs of an occasion. We're taking this a stage further by supplying colourful customised invitations – they can be displayed on noticeboards or make a pleasant souvenir of say, a director's retirement party.'

Your company may never know why they were undercut when they quoted Anniversary Caterers for their illustrated menu cards, and still less why caterers far and wide should have jumped on their bandwagon and developed it to the point of personalised invitations, menu cards, serviettes and 'samples for your children' containers. But let's hope you have some clue why it could have happened, and in future, will remember to beware of that extra drink, and look around for eavesdroppers when you are talking company business in public.

Another occasion where a poorly prepared individual can make a mess of representing his or her organisation is at a formal meeting, where it is often felt that the pressure is on to say something, anything, to make their presence felt.

Never mind that you should not have spoken without having received direct instructions on what to say in favour, or against, a particular point of view. It is almost impossible to button your lip when all around you other people are speaking up for their Heads of Department and apparently making constructive comments.

When in doubt, opt out

You might be lucky and introduce a viewpoint which both impresses the audience and reflects your manager's opinion. On the other hand, you could find yourself on the carpet when, three weeks later, he waves that week's copies of *Fast Food News* and *Quickie Catering Gazette* at you and demands to know who gave you the authority to suggest there was a potential market in providing refreshments for hospital visitors. So that *now* half the caterers in the district had tendered for the concession which had been a private matter for the company to discuss before you let the cat out of the bag.

Getting informed

It follows that whether or not your organisation sets out to brief you before you represent them at any event, you must ask a number of questions to make sure you know what you are supposed to be doing. The same applies in reverse if you are responsible for sending someone to represent you at a function. The casual phrase 'Just as long as we're represented' is tossed around rather too readily in most organisations, without any thought as to the impression that may be given by an inexperienced delegate.

The points to cover in brief (whether you are giving information or seeking it) are first, *why* a particular individual should be chosen. The reasons may range from 'Well, it's on a Thursday and that's always a quiet day for Perks' to 'Perks is the obvious person to send. He knows the computer system inside out and if there does happen to be any software worth having, he'll know which questions to ask.'

It could be, 'Well, there's only Perks. Miss Hill is on holiday, I'm at the Speciality Soups meeting and Ms Heavitree is still struggling to learn "Wordstar."'

The calibre of the candidate will largely dictate what he or she is capable of doing for the organisation at the meeting, exhibition, or demonstration and his or her expertise/limitations should be taken into account. If you are being asked to represent your organisation, this is not an occasion to pretend knowledge and confidence you do not possess. Say, 'I'm glad to be asked to attend in Miss Hill's place, but I've not done anything like this before, and I don't quite know what is expected of me.' That should prompt a clear briefing for you.

Why me? Why there? What for?

The next point to cover is to establish *what* is hoped for as the result of the visit. Is it simply to fly the organisation's flag, in which case all the stand-in has to do is to look good, be pleasant and refrain from drinking too much?

Is it an advertisement for the company, in which case the organisation's representative has to do all these things and make himself known to certain pre-selected clients?

Is the delegate supposed to find anything out? If so, what, and are there any pitfalls to avoid? – shades of the World War II briefing where pilots were warned of danger spots where they might expect flak.

The third point to cover is *how* to prepare for the event. If by chance you are briefing a young employee without a lot of experience, it is important to realise he or she may not know what to wear to different kinds of business event. You might have to be very tactful to make sure an inexperienced person knows how to behave, too.

We all have to learn conventional etiquette and as people get on in business, they can be involved in formal dinners where it can be a hassle to work out which fork or spoon to use for which course or how to eat pâté. Less formally, most young people might be nervous at tackling the buffet served at a press reception or even a training course. It is not easy to cope with plate, glass, package of notes and briefcase or handbag!

Learning from other people's experience

It is often less embarrassing all round if this kind of briefing is done informally between people of near-equal status, rather than from on high by the management. An executive might say to their secretary 'Young Peter Perks is going off to the George Hotel for that sales training course. You might tip him off that most people wear suits and see that he knows the drill for coping at the hotel.' If you are the person being sent to the course or conference, you could seek out someone who is likely to have had the same sort of experience and ask if there is anything they can tell you about the routine.

In the absence of orders to the contrary . . .

There should also be standing orders to cover incidents where instead of being carefully briefed as to his role, the first a stand-in knows of his assignment is when he gets a phone call from someone sounding as if he is about to expire, saying 'You'll have to go to the . . . tomorrow because I'm laid up with flu.' (Or 'stranded at Malaga airport,' or 'dead on my feet after an 18-hour day at the factory, trying to prevent a strike.') Whatever the reason, it is a situation where any employee may be hauled in to represent the organisation at an event they have never experienced

How might you begin planning for such eventualities? First, it should be understood that someone likely to be pitchforked into a demanding meeting or conference is entitled to search the files to see if there is any previous correspondence or reports extant that give an idea of what to expect. A cosy meeting of four delegates can be tougher than minding the stand at a trade exhibition.

Always ask – someone may know

Do not hesitate to seek advice on tactics or behaviour from anyone likely to be 'in the know' about the particular subject. People do like to give advice and provided you do not interrupt them in the middle of some crucial project, but pick your moment to say 'Lisa, I have to represent Victoria Hughs at the meeting with the Meat & Drink Cafe Concessionnaires team. You've taken minutes of previous meetings. Is there anything you can tell me about the actual people so that I don't put my foot in it? And what about the lunch that's arranged? Do I do the ordering, or do they all order their own meals?'

Taking business clients out for a meal is a scary experience for the first time. As a very junior executive, I was once taking my turn on my company's stand at the Motor Show when a frantic senior rushed up to me, pushed a wad of notes into my hand and said 'Those Dutch racing drivers . . . You'll have to give them a meal at . . . (*he named the club*). Taxi them there and back to their hotel and make my apologies.' I was petrified but I got by.

Ask the professionals

If you have to represent your organisation in an unfamiliar setting, you will want to maintain a polite and confident front when dealing with clients or customers or competitors, but you can reasonably ask advice from the professionals. You can ring a hotel and ask them to put a brochure in the post whether you are a holidaymaker or a delegate at a conference. That way you can find out times of meals, get an idea of facilities and see what the place looks like so that it is not entirely unfamiliar.

With a training course, again there is usually an explanatory prospectus to give you an idea what to expect. Or someone else in the company may have taken the same course, or a similar sort of course with a different organisation.

For exhibitions, there are catalogues. Last year's could be a useful guide if there is a copy in the office. Otherwise – well, you do not have to spend the first half hour marching up and down the aisles. You can find the coffee bar and study the catalogue for twenty minutes getting an idea of who is there and what might be interesting to look at.

If you are attending a product or service demonstration, you can read sales literature in advance, make a few notes of points that you want to know about and decide on questions to ask.

'Let me see . . . you are . . . ?'

Names are important. Try and fix them in your mind when you are introduced. If you are representing your organisation at a meeting where delegates sit around a table and make notes, and if you do not know any of the people, do a little sketch to show where each person is sitting and his/her name. Later, as you listen to the different points of view, you can attach personalities to names. When you have turned to the next page in your notebook, make a note of any identifying characteristic that could be important for your organisation to know about. (Miss James – interrupts a lot. Very anxious product range should not be reduced as result of merger. Mrs Cherry – well-informed. Keeps producing statistics and cuttings from magazines. Mr Knight – heavy smoker. **NB** Think this is unpleasant for Mrs Cherry, who keeps turning away from him.) These small points could be very useful to the person who will take your place next time the meeting is held.

At exhibitions and training courses, collect business cards. When you are away from observers, write in pencil on the back anything you want to remember and pass on to senior staff at work. You can always rub it out when it has been noted.

At product demonstrations, make notes on sales literature about prices, delivery dates, servicing agreements, names of existing customers prepared to give their views on the equipment being shown and so on. This is useful to jog your own memory when you are being asked, perhaps several months later, which variety of office printer seemed the best buy.

And the consequence was . . .

Returning to my theme of similarities between military briefing and debriefing sessions, and those held in business and industry, you will recall that the returning pilots were not allowed to have their bacon and egg breakfast until they had been formally debriefed by the intelligence officer. As in war, so in peace – debriefing sessions should be held as soon as possible after the event. It is not always the most important person you remember two or three days after a conference. It is more likely to be the pushy one who kept interrupting, or the delegate who kept cracking jokes, or the one who laughed when you tipped your wine over the carpet.

Don't rely on memory alone

Debriefing, then, should be immediate. If that is not going to be possible and you are the person who expects to have to report back on the meeting, the exhibition or the press conference, do yourself a favour and make a few concise notes. You will probably discover – most of us do – that the handwriting you thought so neat when you were making notes yesterday degenerates rather as the pages go on, and only recent memory makes it possible for you to decipher the last couple of pages. You can see what might happen if you did not bother to read over your notes for a week.

With formal meetings there will be minutes, naming names and saying who said what. With informal meetings, training sessions, large conferences, exhibitions and demonstrations, a helpful typewritten list of names is unlikely to be provided, so write down any useful names in block capitals, so that anyone who needs to can read them.

If the person you have had to represent briefed you well, the debriefing session should be short and pleasant. You know what to look for, how to behave and what questions to ask. You have acquired all this information and facts about names and personalities of those you met.

But suppose you are on the other side of the fence. You were the one who phoned in from Malaga airport and you had little time to tell your stand-in what was required. How do you go about getting the most out of someone else's experience?

Avoid the third degree

First, be pleasant. You are conducting a debriefing session, not an interrogation. Start by thanking the person who stood in for you and then begin with an easy question. 'What was it like at the Fast Foods Fair? Last year I remember it was very crowded.' Get your colleague talking about the atmosphere, about the ease or difficulty of visiting particular stands. You probably need to know where all the attention was focused, but if you ask a direct question like 'Which was the most popular stand? How did our stand compare?' it all starts turning into an examination session and the delegate is inclined to be defensive about his or her observations.

It can be helpful to use a catalogue (or sales brochure, or list of lecture topics, in the case of a training course) when you are debriefing someone who has attended. 'I see that Speciality Soups were offering a "Sip and Savour" bar. Was that a success? Did you get near it?'

Take note of personality quirks

Prompt your representative to talk about people rather than things. You can find out about things from leaflets and books and other users. People's personalities, attitudes and opinions are much more difficult to imagine. Someone who has very recently met Mrs Cherry and can tell you how she kept producing statistics and reports to back up her opinions is invaluable. That information will enable you to be equally well prepared with statistics and reports by the time you meet Mrs Cherry.

You will be glad to have been tipped off about Mr Knight and his pipe, too. Lucky you found this out before you introduced him to your Publicity Director who suffers from asthma. **NB** Substitute the Public Relations Officer for the Publicity Director when meeting Mr Knight.

As you get talking about the personalities of individuals met, so you can find out what they said. Comments like 'Who was it who kept interrupting? What were their main worries, do you suppose?' will extract examples of what was said and an impression of how the interruptions were received.

Keep the conversation flowing

In the average debriefing, the sensitive area is when you are asking someone to say what they said and did when they were replacing you. In order to get accurate information, it is important to stay calm. Even if your eager representative has made some calamitous admission like, 'I don't know about Sip and Savour. Sip and Stagger would be more like it. The chap could hardly stand up and it turned out he was Speciality Soups' Managing Director!' do not wince and turn pale. You need to know whether this less than tactful remark went back to the Speciality Soups' Managing Director, or if he was actually in any state to notice if it had. Control yourself therefore; even try a smile and ask casually 'Who did they have on their stand? Who was the chap you were talking to, for instance?' If nothing else, this brings you to the question of names, and you can start gathering in information on contacts made.

Be encouraging if you can

Praise where you can, criticise only where you must and leave the criticism to the very end. Debriefing is a drawing out of information and of observations that people do not always know they have made until something jogs their memory. In a conversation that is friendly and unhurried, where the other person feels that what he or she has to say is of absorbing interest, they will talk freely. But once someone feels they are under fire, they will batten down the hatches and only say what they feel is safe.

Finally, before you criticise, take into account how well your representative was briefed. (If you are the person receiving criticism, think about this, too, and whether you tried hard enough to prepare yourself for your responsibility.) Doing anything for the first time is quite scary. Doing something for the first time in front of an audience, and conscious that you are only a stand-in for someone who would have been preferred is very demanding. A silly mistake, a rather feeble report back or some other kind of inadequate performance by someone who has just demonstrated the limits of his or her competence may be forgiven. On the other hand, if your representative clearly regarded the day at the Fast Foods Fair as a licence to sample the Bucks Fizz on the first stand, and the Liebfraumilch on the second stand and the catering-size Sangria on the third and eventually had to be poured into a taxi by someone from Speciality Soups, you certainly have every reason to point out the error of their ways. If it does not also prompt you to wonder how you came to make such a crashing mistake in choosing them to attend in the first place, it is time to reconsider your own ability to assess people!

To sum up

Effective briefing and satisfactory debriefing depends on the exchange of useful information, so:

When briefing: Tell stand-ins why they have been chosen, what they can expect to happen and what they should and should not do. Remind them to protect the organisation's interests.

When being briefed: Ask why you have been chosen; what is expected of you and how you can prepare. Find out in advance any information on what may happen, how to behave and prepare to take notes.

When debriefing: Do it as soon as possible after the event. Avoid interrogating people; encourage them to talk about people you missed meeting, rather than facts you can chase up. Praise effort, make allowances for inexperience.

When being debriefed: Answer questions fully and add any extra observations you think could be useful. Be accurate about names and reported comments. Admit any mistakes you may have made so your organisation may prepare for and answer criticisms!

8 Meetings and how to manage them

- What are the responsibilities when organising a meeting?
- In what order do you tackle the tasks?
- How can you space out the discussions to give everyone a chance to speak?
- What are minutes?

What do you mean, you do not know how to manage a meeting? If you have ever organised a party, or even been a guest at one, you are aware of some of the skills needed to get the right people together in the right place at the right time.

A meeting is, in effect, a business party; a get-together of people concerned with, or affected by, the same thing. At first it may seem strange to make a comparison between a party and a meeting, but as we can see for ourselves from radio and TV programmes, the 'confrontational' style of meeting often ends with the comment 'talks broke up at 10 p.m. after the two sides failed to reach agreement.' How much better to aim for a warm and friendly atmosphere, and hear that 'discussions between the two sides were amicable and a settlement is expected shortly.'

Whether you are organising a meeting between your organisation and another one, or an inter-office meeting to talk over a departmental problem, or perhaps taking part in a meeting on your organisation's behalf for the first time, you will find it repays all the efforts you may choose to put in towards making it a pleasant and stress-free event.

Be prepared to co-operate

You cannot avoid all tension and stress. Some meetings are on sensitive subjects or deal with emotive situations like sacking people or closing down an operation. Some delegates may be anxious, perhaps because the result of the meeting will affect their future or simply because they have never been to a meeting in a responsible capacity before.

94

You can reduce tensions by ensuring that any factor likely to make the meeting run more smoothly is taken care of. These factors can range from making sure the meeting is held in an accessible place (so that no delegate arrives tired and crochety, or worse, late, after an awkward journey) to providing a clear agenda, so that all concerned can prepare points to discuss.

Make sure you are thoroughly briefed

If you are someone attending an important meeting for the first time, this question of advance preparation is very important for you. As with all new experiences, it pays to find out as much about the general procedure as you can by talking to people who have attended similar meetings before you go along. You want to be able to concentrate on what is said, not be worrying over whether you are supposed to stand up to address the group. Ask around your office and look through files which give details of previous meetings with this group of people so that you can find clues as to what you might expect.

If you are given the responsibility of co-ordinating the arrangements for a meeting, there are five questions that must be answered. If they are fully explained, your meeting should achieve something.

Have a realistic objective

Do not take it for granted that a single meeting will resolve all problems. It may take several meetings to arrive at a decision. Often enough meetings are held to decide on the sort of action that may help people reach a decision eventually. There are often meetings held simply to introduce people to one another – two companies may hope to work together, for example.

Why? Who? When? Where? How?

These are the five crucial questions to get answered when you are involved in organising a meeting. The more detailed the answers, the more likely your meeting is to be successful. Small matters, like who sits next to whom can be important. (Smokers should be separated from non smokers for instance.) Indeed, that particular point could turn out to be crucial. If you ask in advance if there is any objection to smoking being permitted at the meeting, you may find that Mr Knight is a compulsive smoker. On the other hand, Mrs Cherry is prone to asthma. One or other of these two might need to be replaced by a well-briefed stand-in.

Setting the scene

Why is the meeting being held? You need to discover this in order to ensure that the right people (*Who?*) are invited. It could also have a bearing on the timing of the meeting (*When?*) as there is not much point in meeting to discuss something when it is too late for any agreed action to affect the issue. The location (*Where?*) a meeting is held could be important for practical reasons; you must pick somewhere everyone can reach.

There may be tactical reasons too. 'You want *me* to come to *your* headquarters?' demands the client. 'That will mean staying overnight in Wakefield. Why can't we meet half way – Birmingham, for instance?' (But you may want that client to see over your premises in Wakefield as, once they recognise all you have to offer, their acceptance of your tender is much more likely.) In this sort of situation, assuring them that you will be pleased to arrange and cover the costs of accommodation near your headquarters may solve the problem.

Videoconference facilities

When the people taking part in a meeting are based far apart, you might investigate British Telecom's 'Confravision' system. People taking part in a 'videoconference' can use public videoconference rooms in London, Birmingham, Manchester, Bristol, Belfast, Aberdeen, Glasgow, Ipswich and Douglas, I.o.M. These rooms provide a display camera through which text, graphics, charts and documents can be shown to six people, on average, who can see each other via video screens in their different locations. Some centres have overflow facilities for additional people to watch and hear the conference from outside the videoconference room.

BT launched the world's first international videoconferencing service in 1984. There are links between the UK and Canada, the USA, the Federal Republic of Germany, the Netherlands, France and Belgium with other countries coming on stream. To find out more about the BT national and/or international videoconferencing systems, ring the number(s) quoted for conference call enquiries at the front of your local phone book.

You can see that the *How?* of arranging a meeting is to make it as convenient, pleasant and rewarding an experience for everyone as you can possibly manage, wherever it is to be held. Once you are lucky enough to get agreement from all the right people to be in the right place at the right time, you must ensure it has all the equipment needed to make a fruitful use of the time allocated. To illustrate the importance of each of the five factors listed, here is how they could affect companies in general, and two of the 'invented' firms we have met – Gammon, Hambone, Porkpie and Brawn and Pressed Pork Products.

Why is the meeting being held? Perhaps because there are matters that need to be discussed face to face rather than by phone or in an exchange of letters. This may be because they involve a number of people, and it is far too complicated and time-consuming to wait for each participant in turn to send in his or her views.

Confidentiality – from the start

It might be because the matters to be discussed deal with developments that are of very great value to competitors, so that progress needs to be kept confidential with the minimum put on paper. Knowledge of the project is limited to those at the meeting.

The most common reason for a meeting is to organise a project. Earlier in this book, the idea was mooted of a merger between Gammon, Hambone, Porkpie and Brawn, and Pressed Pork Products. You might expect that because they have a basic commodity – pork – in common, there could be a lot to discuss. How do the two product ranges compare? Will the new company need the same number of production outlets and production staff? What will each firm gain and lose, financially and in terms of reputation and customers? These could be just a few of the questions to be discussed at a meeting between principals of the two companies.

Almost certainly such a proposed merger would need to be discussed with the shareholders. Equally concerned will be the trade unions as their members' jobs could be affected. Meetings could be necessary with several groups of people, and at several stages of the project. For example, at some stage, the newly merged company will need to notify the press and seek publicity for the merger. A meeting will be needed with the company's own public relations team and any agency they may retain to produce an advertising campaign, new logo, packaging design; even revamped letter headings.

'Why?' (Introducing Choice Pork Products)

For the purpose of working through the *Who, When, Where* and *How* stages of managing a meeting, this chapter assumes that the merger between Gammon, Hambone *et al* and Pressed Pork Products is going to go ahead, and they are getting together to decide on a new image for the company, which they have already agreed to call Choice Pork Products.

Next they have to consider whether they should go ahead with an independent launch for the new company (which Gammon, Hambone favours) or whether they should spend money on the professional services of a design consultancy. Pressed Pork Products have always used an outside company called Attention Seekers to handle their promotions, design their logo, regularly update their packaging design and organise their presence at exhibitions. A meeting to discuss the pros and cons of either method has to be held, and it will be hosted by Gammon, Hambone.

It is a convention that the organisation that hosts a meeting undertakes all the detailed work of setting it up, so someone from Gammon, Hambone will be responsible for contacting those who are to be invited and making it as easy as possible for each person to attend.

'Who?'

Suppose you are the organiser. Your first task should be to find out who *must* attend the meeting. Probably in this case, it would be the Marketing Manager of your own company, the Advertising Manager of your own company and the Marketing Manager of Pressed Pork Products. The Marketing Manager of Pressed Pork Products might well feel outnumbered and suggest that the Creative Director of Attention Seekers should come along with some ideas for a new logo and packaging design to match the new company's image. This brings in an outsider, so it would have to be discussed with your own Marketing Manager.

Getting the go-ahead for a project of this kind is unusual without it being carefully costed, so it would not be unusual for both Gammon, Hambone and Pressed Pork Products to want an executive from their financial teams at the meeting. (In setting this particular scene, we are assuming that no one has been made redundant yet, but because it is on the cards, you could well find that both Marketing Managers and both Finance Managers will be defending their own corners vigorously.) As for the sole Advertising Manager, from Gammon, Hambone, you can be sure she is determined to come along thoroughly prepared to tackle the threat of much of her work being put out to a consultancy.

'When?'

As meeting organiser, your first move needs to be to contact your company's potential delegates, and get from them as wide a choice of possible dates as they can manage for the meeting. Often enough you will find that if everyone gives you three possible dates, one is acceptable to each person you have asked, and perhaps one other might just be managed with a bit of effort.

You then get on to the other potential delegates, bearing in mind that though Gammon, Hambone's team may not have objected to the presence of the Creative Director from Attention Seekers at some stage, this first meeting could be held without him. It is a good tactic, as well as good manners, to start off by asking to speak to the secretary to the Marketing Manager of Pressed Pork Products.

Establishing lines of communication

Secretaries usually maintain their executives' diaries and can, if they choose, tell you which dates appear to be free. In any event, it is important for someone organising a meeting to get on good terms with all the secretaries and assistants who might be involved. The Marketing Manager will not want to be constantly called to the phone to be asked if he needs car parking booked for him at the hotel, or if he is coming by train and needs to be met; if he would mind starting just one hour earlier than planned because the small conference room is needed for another meeting, and so on and so forth. Queries of this kind are best dealt with in one answering session rather than by constant interruption.

100

Like a party, the meeting will be more successful if it is organised to suit all the guests, not just the home team. You need to give your contact(s) a choice of dates: by all means, emphasise the one that is most convenient, but provide alternatives.

'Where?'

You will have been told the location of the meeting but it will almost certainly be necessary to book space. It would be unusual for the organisation hosting a meeting to go to another company's premises for it, but it is quite usual for neutral ground to be chosen, such as a hotel.

Here you can run into snags. It is embarrassing to discover (after you have patiently waited, argued and persuaded all your participants to agree on a particular day and time) that the hotel you usually use for meetings is booked up. The wise planner does a little phoning round on a tentative basis whilst waiting for a reply from the people expected to attend the meeting.

Obviously, you will try your favourite hotel first. You probably know the person who takes bookings for conference rooms and he or she will understand that any booking has to be provisional. On the other hand, if you discover on this first call that the place is booked solid with a sales training course for the first week in which you have provisional dates, and a package tour for the second, you are in trouble. You will need to look further afield and see which other hotels might have conference rooms where your meeting can be held.

When in doubt, ask

At this point, seek guidance from your immediate senior or the executive on whose behalf you are fixing the meeting. It may be an occasion when the company board room could be used in order to avoid going to an exceptionally expensive hotel (which happens to be the only one with a free conference room, and which might give the visiting delegates the idea you are trying to overawe them). You should avoid causing unintentional anxiety or suspicion by explaining difficulties over booking space.

In this imperfect world, few dates ever suit everyone. You will probably end up with a compromise, and it could be, for instance, that the Creative Director from Attention Seekers cannot attend the meeting at all, though he can make lunch. This is an arrangement worth going for if all concerned agree; sometimes it is an advantage simply to get to know someone before you decide whether to talk hard facts with them, and it could be to everyone's advantage to share an after-meeting lunch.

Meanwhile, there is the little matter of organising accommodation. Assuming you have arrived at a date and time that suits the participants, you now have to arrange everything with the hotel that had a suitable room free.

Perhaps you know everything there is to know about this hotel already: what the car parking is like; which conference room you have been allocated; how to organise refreshments; whether you need to book lunch for your group; and of course, what they can provide in the way of conference equipment, whether it is a projector and screen to show a set of slides plus notepads and pens for making notes, or something more elaborate like an interpreter. (This meeting may not need one, but a future one with French or Chinese importers might.)

'Check it out'

Even if you are going to the hotel three streets away which you always use, it is worth 'checking it out'. You cannot possibly go and inspect every conference room before you make a booking, but if it is easy to go and look, do so. Is there building work going on that will deafen and irritate participants? And what's this? They have closed the ladies' toilet on the conference floor for renovation? You had better find out where there is a convenient convenience before the meeting gets under way.

If you cannot inspect the venue because it is too far away, collect as much literature as possible and ask questions about anything that could be important. Imagine yourself as a delegate. What would you need to know about? How can you make it easy for people to be directed to the right room? (In a big hotel, there may be a board in the foyer which shows where each meeting is being held.) Would you like one break mid-morning and perhaps another one to chat over an aperitif?

The value of breaking up meetings at pre-arranged times is that if the discussion is being held back by an argument that cannot be solved there and then, the break gives you the chance to restart on a fresh topic.

'How?'

The last task in organising a meeting is that of planning the agenda and taking minutes. The agenda is a formal way of setting down what you hope will be discussed. The minutes are a formal way of recording what was actually discussed. Each person invited to the meeting should be identified on the agenda, with his or her name, job title and parent organisation. In the minutes, everyone who is quoted should be similarly identified in this way the first time they speak. Subsequent comments only need to identify them by name.

Ideally each heading on the agenda should be covered at the meeting and also be referred to in the minutes. It may not always work out like that, or, if it does, the reference may be limited to: 'Mrs Cherry hoped the matter of redeploying the former merchandisers as demonstrators (held over due to lack of time) would be discussed as a matter of urgency at the next meeting. This was agreed by all present.'

Timing and tactics

In planning the agenda for a meeting, it helps to make allowance for the fact that time goes very slowly at the start and then gradually speeds up until, as the end of the meeting approaches, it is galloping at such a rate there often seems no way of fitting everything in. (In this respect, business meetings are very like many parties. So, just as you would not book the entertainers or the singing telegram for the first half hour of a party, do not insert the most crucial discussion points as the first item on the agenda!)

It pays to design an agenda so that the important discussion can be reached about an hour or so into the meeting. By then everyone will have settled down and taken the measure of everyone else; people will have started to remember other people's names and gain an impression of individual personalities.

Strategic refreshment breaks

Anything likely to spark off violent argument should be placed before the coffee break. You may be very glad of an excuse to break up a discussion that is getting nowhere, or perhaps even to have the chance to take someone who is losing his or her cool on one side. Many unforgivable blasts of crossfire may be averted by a quiet word like, 'We're going to need a separate discussion on this matter, don't you agree? I liked your point about . . . but the whole business needs more time than we can give it in a general meeting like this one.'

Opportunities for each participant to speak should be sprinkled through the agenda like currants in a bun. There is little point in inviting someone to a meeting unless they have a chance to speak, but shyer people may need to be provoked by the necessity to make a point.

Invitations to speak

In the sort of meeting we are considering, it is unlikely that anyone from the Marketing or Advertising Department might need urging to come forward, as presentation is (or should be) their forte. On the other hand, if Gammon, Hambone have brought along their Finance Director, and alas, Pressed Pork Products' Finance Director is in Egypt, their Finance Manager is off sick and her assistant has never attended this sort of meeting before, he must be made to say something, even if it is that he does not have the authority to make a decision. Otherwise, when the question of financing the promotion is still hanging fire, people may not remember why an agreement could not be reached.

This brings us conveniently to the matter of minutes – recording what people said at the meeting. If by some rare chance, Gammon, Hambone and Pressed Pork Products should want every single utterance recorded, they will have to book either a tape recorder or a court shorthand writer. Nowadays, secretaries with the very high shorthand speed needed to undertake such a task are rarely found.

A matter of record

It is more usual for the minutes to record the sense of someone's remark and, of course, who that someone was. In case you skipped the suggestion that when attending a meeting with people who are new to you, you should make a little sketch map to refresh your memory about their names and job titles.

Having attended many meetings, the secret of success seems to be in the personality of the Chairperson (which is the word that seems to have replaced 'Chairman' or 'Chairwoman'. In some cases, the word you have to use is 'Chair').

To be good at chairing meetings, you need the charisma of a TV personality; the cloak of invisibility of a chameleon; the peripheral vision of an airline pilot and the built-in time sense of a nurse or teacher. In that way you will be able to lead and control your restive team, merge into the background when fruitful discussion needs to be encouraged, spot the outsider trying to get a word in and break up the general chat when it is time to move on. Probably the skills that make a good chairperson are inborn; they are certainly unforgettable once observed, but they can be noted and gradually acquired.

Co-operating for results

What makes a good chairperson into a perfect chairperson is the ability to notice the unfortunate minute-taker, who is listening intently and desperately trying to do a precis of a lengthy speech with many interruptions, and note down who made which point. The chairperson who tactfully suggests that such-and-such a summing up might be made, or who halts the meeting so that the minute-taker can catch up, deserves every praise. Such people are so rare that the novice minute-taker is well advised to approach any chairperson in advance and say 'May I sit beside you or opposite you, so that I can catch your eye if I need help or advice at any stage during the meeting.'

The minute-taker will be a help to the chairperson if he or she has a watch on the table where it is easily seen, so that the time at which each point on the agenda is reached, and the time when discussion concludes, can be noted down. This way the minute-taker can keep an eye on how effectively points are being covered. If the meeting is running seriously behind, then during the break the chairperson's attention can be drawn to the problem and you may both decide to carry over some parts of the agenda to another meeting.

Instant action and effective presentation

Minutes should always be typed up immediately after the meeting. This is not only because your memory might fade after a few days and that squiggle you used becomes incomprehensible to you or any of your group's delegates, but other people present may forget exactly who said what, and if they do not get their copy of the minutes very soon afterwards, they may claim you have got it all wrong. 'They didn't say that; it was someone else. And anyway, the emphasis of the minutes isn't correct: they were pushed into such-and-such a decision.' You can see how easy it is for awkward people to take up such views if they have to wait ten days for their copy of the minutes of the meeting.

Never forget the little courtesies. People like to read that the delegates were welcomed to the meeting by Robert Cust and that it was agreed that a useful point was contributed by Lisa Hardy. Sometimes when you read in the minutes 'A long, and obviously carefully prepared report was contributed by Tom Lloyd', you may think to yourself 'Ah, Tom went on and on again as usual.' But if you want Tom's commitment to your project, this is more tactful than omitting reference to his comments, or worse, using the word 'lengthy'.

To sum up

To organise a meeting that people will attend willingly, participate in fully and come to reasonable decisions that they will later implement, you need to:

- Understand the purpose of the meeting
- Invite the right people
- Find an acceptable location and time
- Ensure the comfort of delegates
- Prepare and circulate a clear agenda
- Give every participant the chance to speak
- Keep a progress check at the meeting
- Identify contributors when recording minutes
- Prepare and circulate minutes soon after the meeting

9 Coping with pressures

- What are the causes of office pressures?
- How can you spot stress building up?
- What avoidable hazards can you tackle?
- When can action prevent tension?
- How can you cope with change?

The most dangerous kind of pressure is the kind that builds up slowly. Sudden surges of work, like extra demands related to the launch of a new product, or unexpected challenges, such as the absence of a key person, can spur people on to cope. They will collaborate to get the work done and take a positive pride in managing, despite the difficulties.

Identifying stresses

Explosions are most likely to occur when the pressure is insidious. Perhaps there is one person who never pulls his or her weight and holds everybody else's work up. Perhaps the office is under-equipped for the volume of work that has to be done. There may be an old-fashioned system in operation that needs to be overhauled because the content of work has changed.

People get used to 'making do' when they feel they cannot afford the time to stop and reorganise. Of course it would be better to have half a dozen neatly clipped piles of documents instead of that great tumbling heap of letters, circulars, magazines, reports and memos. It is just that there are no bulldog clips, and to indent for them means filling in a form in duplicate and getting it signed, and then finding someone who will take it along to stores. Or, in a small firm, remembering to get the petty cash and add 'bulldog clips' to your list when you go out to the stationery shop.

Adding to the load

Then there is the question of people who do not do their fair share of the work. There may be a good reason to make allowances for those in training, or nearing retirement, or with home problems. However, accepting that everyone will make allowances for Miss X or Mr Y does not solve the problem of the work left undone. A way must be found to cope, maybe by sharing out the extra work before it clogs up the office routine and makes everyone resentful.

Routine – now there is another possible source of aggravation and pressure. If you are the person who types the invoices every Thursday, but your work depends on getting copies of orders sent out by Wednesday evening, and you are regularly kept waiting for some of them until Thursday afternoon, sooner or later your patience will snap. You may need to change your routine. For instance, have it agreed that all invoices will be sent out on Thursday provided that you receive all copy orders by Wednesday. All others will be held over to the following Thursday – not left to drag on through Friday.

Releasing tension

Organising that sort of scheme will call for both time and tact. It is fatal to leave a situation of pressure until you are so stressed and overworked that you blow your top, tossing the orders down on your desk, saying 'type the invoices yourself, then!' and storming off to smoke or cry in the loo. Removing yourself from the stress situation is not a bad idea. Unless you work for a military-style organisation, where staff may be forbidden to leave the base during working hours, there is a lot to be said for absenting yourself from the scene of action for fifteen minutes and going for a brisk walk round the block until you cool down. It beats loosing your temper and few routines are so rigid that you cannot disappear for a while. Better still, though, how can you prevent office pressures simmering away until one day 'PSST!' everything blows up?

Keep looking out for trouble

An efficient office, like a happy classroom or a successful shop, is not a place of hushed voices, firm commands and anxious glances at the clock to make sure you are meeting deadlines. The ideal is that everyone has enough work to keep them absorbed, sufficient variety of work to offer a challenge and some control over the order in which they do their work so that the 'treadmill' effect of doing the same dreary old things every day can be avoided.

Achieving the right balance is not easy, particularly as far as the variety is concerned. If you are an office manager and Mr Tibble is the best word-processing operator in the place, it is natural to think of him for all the really demanding w.p. jobs – like the vital but hideously boring catalogue with its list of prices and sizes, particularly if it has to be updated every month and it would take so long to train someone else.

Mayday! Mayday!

If you do fall into this trap, however, there is a very good chance that one day (if you are lucky) Mr Tibble will ask to see you and say that his job is driving him mad with frustration and he feels he must leave. If you are unlucky, you will get a month's notice and a request for a reference for the new job that he has been offered. Then you really will have a problem in training someone else to produce the catalogue.

Similarly if you are the kind of boss who always picks the phone up when it rings, even when you have a secretary to receive your calls, and then, just as she is confirming that you have a note in your diary about the meeting, you chip in and say, 'Hi, Mrs Cherry. Bill Summers here. Mr Knight won't be coming. I know how you feel about that pipe of his' . . . do not be too surprised if one day she switches the phone permanently through to your extension and lets you get on with it.

There are all kinds of other irritations concerned with people that can rub away at others' patience until something sparks off an undignified row, or worse, loses a really worthwhile member of staff: the person who always takes the last large padded envelope from the stationery cupboard and does not remind the stationery clerk to order more; the borrower (of the stapler, the sellotape, the address book) who never puts anything back in the right place; the person who arranges dental appointments for 11.30 so that it is not worth coming in in the morning, and turns up at 2.30 complaining that the injection still has not worn off.

Sounds familiar?

As you can see, like the man in *The Mikado*, I've got a little list, and I dare say I appear on someone else's list somewhere, too. But rather than let exasperating behaviour of this kind drag on until it festers, you should take action.

This does not always mean a stand-up fight. Indeed, if you do as this section suggests and keep looking out for trouble, you will spot tensions before they have a chance to build up.

Action stations

If you bother to notice people's expressions, you will know how Mr Tibble feels about word-processing that catalogue before it has a chance to drive him out of the job. Instead of letting him put up with it until he can stand it no longer, you can say 'Mr Tibble. You make a marvellous job of the catalogue and it's tempting to ask you to do it every month but that wouldn't be fair because it's such a chore. What do you feel about trusting young Gill to amend some of the prices? If we take her off checking orders, she'll have the time, and it could be good training?' That way, you should get everyone's co-operation.

The executive who picks up the phone to see if it is being answered correctly, or whether it is someone he or she wants to talk to is a trickier problem. If you are getting exasperated by it, you can see what happens if you interrupt in your turn, 'Oh, Mrs Davies. I'll pass you over to Mr Summers now.' Or try it the other way, 'Oh Mr Summers. I didn't know you wanted to talk to Mrs Davies. I'll put my receiver down.' A reasonably sensitive soul who values your services will take the hint.

You could also try a more direct attack. 'May I speak to you, Mr Summers? I'm worried because whenever I answer your phone, you pick up the extension. Am I doing something wrong?' Or, 'Mr Summers, would you like me to switch your calls straight through today. I get the impression you may be waiting for a particular call.'

If Mr Summers does not see from that that his next phone call will be to the job centre for your replacement, it is worth one last try to say that you find it embarrassing to be listened to and corrected during your conversations. However, none of us like direct criticism, so if you are going to do this, recognise that he may erupt and say 'I'll answer my phone when I like, and you'll just have to put up with it.' At this point, you may feel it is worth checking what the job centre has to offer.

Preventive measures

Where people pressures are concerned, it is usually far better to try and get round the problem than tackle one individual head-on. In your stationery cupboard, towards the bottom of any supply of paper, envelopes, carbon, etc. put a card 'RUNNING OUT – PLEASE REORDER NOW!' With the borrower, make one person responsible for the items that keep going missing and have a notebook in which they can write down who borrowed what and when. As far as the determined absentee is concerned, a memo to all staff, asking them to make every effort to make medical, dental and optical appointments before 10 a.m. or after 4 p.m. otherwise pay may be affected, can work wonders. Make sure you clear this with the trade union, if there is one, first of all. And be reasonable. If yours is an office to which people commute, it might be fairer to say 'appointments to allow for either a morning, or an after-noon's work'. You are not out to crack the whip, just to save the loss of a whole day unless someone's really unwell.

What if the tension in your office is caused by someone who frankly is bone idle? Well, it is difficult to get rid of such a person and on the whole, employment law protects the employee rather than the employer, which is probably the way it should be if there has to be a bias. No one wants a situation where the lone individual has no defence against the large company.

Broken reeds

But deliberate laziness, taking you all for a ride as opposed to inefficiency (which you can cure with training) needs to be tackled. Anyone pursuing a determined policy of nonco-operation deserves to get just that. It is worth testing the water to see whether the apparent laziness is because of boredom. Try the person on a challenging but non-urgent job, so that if they make a mess, it is not a disaster. And of course, you will already have checked whether the person is ill, or has some home trouble that distracts them from work.

But when you are left with laziness, there are various courses of action. First, inform the lazy person that you know what is happening and give examples of missed work or poor performance. Make it clear that unless there is an improvement, there will certainly be no salary increase or opportunity for promotion and that you may have to take the complaint further.

Let colleagues know you are aware of the problems they have with a lazy member of staff. At the same time, single out hard-working staff for encouragement, giving them interesting work and/or privileges that you do not offer to the lazy member of staff. This will make the lazy person stop and think 'Why not me? Why am I missing out on these opportunities?' But do not be unpleasant to the idler – it is true that you catch more flies with sugar than with vinegar. Some people slip into lazy ways because they have had slapdash supervision, or because they have come from an office where the pace was so slow that they expected to be bored. With this type of person, once they see other members of staff getting all the interesting tasks and earning extra concessions, they will often decide to try a bit harder, particularly if the alternative is to change jobs and perhaps find themselves in an even more demanding position. Watch out for any improvement in their performance and remark upon it.

Patching things up

Praise efforts. I will say that again because it is important. Praise efforts. This is just as vital for the efficient employees of this world as the lazy junior who actually manages to get in on time two mornings in succession. We all like to be appreciated and far too often the good people get resentful because they are taken for granted.

This goes for bosses as well. You may have had a battle royal over the telephones with Mr Summers, but that is no reason not to thank him for showing you how to put a set of minutes together, or to admire his choice of the new cover design for the catalogue. Bosses need cheering up too!

Train before you need it

Once upon a time, small firms would lure already trained staff from big firms which could afford to run training schemes. I do not say it does not still go on, but efforts to make training more widely available to every size of firm make it possible for most companies to be more independent. Nowadays there are evening courses and distance learning courses as well as training packages that can be bought or borrowed to use on the firm's premises. This is a good thing for everyone, not just the big firms who used to lose their trained staff to competitors.

For a start, if you are in charge of the training, you can see it meets the specific needs of your organisation, now and in the future. You might use a standard training package, and build your own internal training course around it, making use of quiet times like Monday mornings or Friday afternoons. You can offer free introductory courses in some aspect of office work, like Speedwriting or Audiotyping, in the lunch hour.

The hurdles that are often most difficult to get over are first the employer's unwillingness to provide training for anyone who does not actually need it at that moment ('Why should I train Mr Tibble in telephone sales? He'll only leave for a better job, and then who will type the catalogue?'); and then, surprisingly, the office staff's unwillingness to learn things not actually needed for the job they are doing.

Room for improvement

Some people see it as a criticism when they are selected for a training course. I know exactly what this feels like as it once happened to me. After I had been presenting a radio programme for several weeks, I was told I had been selected for a training scheme for radio presenters. Instead of saying sensibly 'Oh, good. Now I can find out how the experts do it', I reacted by saying 'But I haven't done anything wrong, have I? Why do *I* have to take a course?' Very stupid, as I discovered when I found out the names of several very successful radio and TV presenters who had been delighted by the opportunity to improve their skills. Memo, never reject the chance to learn new skills or improve existing ones.

Mind you, there is a happy medium between the 'my work is my all' school of thought, and the 'I'm paid from nine to five, and that's what I'll work' fraternity. Think hard if you are the boss before you take up more than two evenings a week of your employee's time. If you are the potential trainee, ask yourself if you are going to be able to stay the course before the employer pays for it. If you are doubtful, find out if there is a less demanding or shorter alternative.

But adding extra skills to your own battery of abilities, or giving your staff this chance means that if someone leaves abruptly, you can step in to the breach and maybe earn promotion, or if you are the employer, you can get by until either you take on another telephone sales person/ accounts clerk/ VAT expert, or have someone partly trained on to an intensive course.

Warning! Overload! Breakdown imminent . . .

Right at the beginning of this chapter I referred to pressure building up insidiously and the danger of explosion. Explosion can come in many forms; most dramatically by the workforce in the office downing tools, or one crucial person walking out. It may be less obvious if people start to be off sick a lot, or you find constant errors in their work. Or you feel that people are unenthusiastic when you announce a new project.

All these are alarm signals. Act on them at once by asking those most likely to be affected by overload if there is a problem and what it is – lack of staff, lack of facilities, lack of system.

If it is lack of staff, going to an agency for a 'temp' is a good idea, and the sooner the better. It is so much easier for a temporary member of staff to be eased gently into the job by someone already doing it than to find they are at a strange desk doing something of which they only have a rough idea. 'Panic early, and panic good' if it is a staff shortage problem. If you spot that there are regular work surges, think ahead and try to book the same temp to come in at these times.

Too few hours in the day

Time pressures can also cause a build-up that leads to an explosion. The person unlucky enough to be the fifth one to interrupt you in the middle of a job that needs concentration may get the full blast of it. The boss who nags with unimportant little queries when you are trying to concentrate on a set of statistics or hunting a mistake in a computer print-out could well get an answer that is more than they bargained for.

In Chapter 2, *Planning and priorities*, there is advice on time management and dealing with priorities. Something worth repeating is to look at your day and your week and decide where the fixed points are. Which jobs must be done at a certain time? Which jobs demand your full concentration?

Once you know this, you can plan ahead. With the time-related jobs, you can work backwards so that all the information you need to do the job properly arrives in good time. You can get people into a routine so that they know you will be doing invoices on Thursday and it is no good asking you to do other tasks.

With the jobs that demand concentration, you could arrange for someone else to handle all phone calls (or put your answering machine on, if you are self-employed). If you are a boss, you may well have a secretary who will keep callers off your back. If not, make sure everyone you work with knows that you have this particular job that needs concentration and ask them ahead of time if there is anything they want you to do before you start. It is a way of warning that you are going to need an uninterrupted spell of work but it shows that you want to be helpful too.

The other thing you can do is look for unused time in the week and time your crucial work for that. Come in early on a Monday. Work through a Friday lunch hour. Make an official arrangement that you stay late on a particular night for a particular job, and can take time off *in lieu* on another day. Many employers are only too willing to invent their own version of 'flexitime' for someone obviously keen to solve a time pressure problem with an idea of their own.

The photocopier has jammed again!

Equipment failure or hold-ups due to lack of supplies are situations almost guaranteed to make office staff blow their tops. It really is the giddy limit when the printer takes to leaving six spaces between every word in the middle of a vital report; or the idiot at the photocopier constantly prints copies that are just off-centre, or the answering machine gives you back half messages. Consulting your Office Notebook you can call in the service expert at once, but that may not be soon enough if he or she has to travel some distance to get to you. Also service engineers are not usually sitting around waiting for calls.

So what do you do? Have a little rant by all means. Life is unfair. You came in early to do this job and now look, sixteen spoilt sheets and goodness knows when you will be able to restart. Tell it all to the wall in the cloakroom or the empty air as you walk round the block. Then you will be able to think of a plan.

In the case of the printer, have you overlooked something? Perhaps if you went back and read the instructions carefully again . . . And that stand-in at your usual photocopying service is never going to be able to do what you want. Why not cut your losses and try another photocopying service? Whilst you are there, pick up some literature on

116

office photocopiers. You may be a small business but perhaps it will be an economy in the end to invest in your own photocopying equipment.

Second opinion

Those half messages on the answering machine. Listen to them again, preferably with a colleague who may supply clues. 'That call about rabbits! I'll bet that was from Bunnies' Childminding Service. Don't you remember? They enquired about Dozy Duvets in small sizes, and with rabbit-patterned covers?' Or 'There was something that sounded like Kennan in that last message. Could that be Mr Kennan of Beady Eye Detectives? You know, the chap with the husky voice.'

Be prepared for change

If you ever fill in magazine questionnaires on the subject of stress, you will know that one of the factors that can be very stressful is changing your job. OK, so you know that and you have no intention of leaving the firm where you like everyone.

But jobs can change from within – your firm is about to merge. It is most unlikely that the two firms have always worked in the same way. There could be storms ahead if you are not prepared for this and willing to have an open mind about new ways of working that might be suggested to you.

If you are self-employed, success can force change upon you. It might have suited you very well to get up at 6 a.m. and do all your paperwork before you call the children for school so that you can machine away at your Dozy Duvets between 9.30 and 3. But orders are pouring in from all sides. The paperwork is spilling over to the machining time and you are losing even more of that because you have to go round and see outworkers, some of whom cannot do the work half as well as you do yourself. Oh dear, oh dear, change is rearing its head again.

These situations are less painful if all concerned take part in the change. It is having change imposed on you that is so unnerving; you do not know what to expect. Let's say you are the Dozy Duvets proprietor. You have to go and visit the outworkers and you need to do it before they have mangled another batch of duvet covers. How about straight after taking the children to school? And, if you start work at 6 a.m., how would it be if you had brunch at 11 a.m. so you could work straight through with just a tea break until you leave to pick the children up from school at 3 p.m.?

Draw up comparisons

With the merger, you need to identify differences and similarities between the way in which your particular job is tackled at the other company. Find a piece of paper and draw a line down the middle. Head it with the name of the job, such as, 'Invoices'. On one side, put how you handle them. On the other how the other firm operates. Once you look at the situation, you could find it is not really that much more of a hassle to send an extra (pink) copy invoice to market research for their survey, or to calculate the exact weight of the order for transportation records. Your initial panic about sheaves of paper and columns of figures was perhaps a bit overdone. When you show your work to the boss (also facing change, remember), he or she will probably indent for a calculator for you in sheer relief.

To sum up

To cope effectively with pressures at work you need to:

- Combat stress – take a break rather than fly off the handle
- Identify the problem – is it people, time, equipment or what?
- Identify the cause of the problem – can you solve it?
- Try various solutions with the help from colleagues
- Train or be trained, to avoid skills shortages
- Reorganise working methods to prevent stress
- Accept changes calmly; they could be for the better

10 Equipping and staffing the office

- What are the essential purchases when setting up an office?
- Where can you save money?
- When does 'image' matter?
- Can you work at your home or must you rent offices?
- How do you choose good staff?

If you are joining, or already working in a big company's offices, you may feel this chapter is not very relevant to your situation. Think again. Not only might you decide one day to set up in business for yourself, but simply knowing what is involved in equipping and staffing an office will give you an insight into the responsibilities of management and that is no bad thing for anyone who is ambitious.

If you are setting up in business for yourself, this chapter should help you get your priorities right. It can be tempting to skim through an office products catalogue, deciding you will have this elegant twelve-drawer filing system or that matching set of address book, diary and blotter. Fortunately, lack of capital preserves the average entrepreneur from the worst extravagances, but if you know little about equipping an office, it is easy to make the wrong choices.

As Chapter 5 emphasised, an office is primarily a centre for communication, so when you are equipping your office, you need to begin with the items that will enable people to reach you.

Basic needs

You will need notepaper (printing firms often call this 'letter heading') with the name, address and phone number of your firm clearly printed. If yours is a limited company, and you have called it something else other than your own name, you will also need to include the names of the directors on your headed notepaper. Other information you might have to include by law is the company registration number, and, if you are registered for VAT, your VAT number.

So much for what you might have to put on your notepaper. It may be quite a lot to fit in neatly already. However, if the business you are in is not clear from the firm's name, you may need an extra line describing your trade or profession. John & Mary Parker, Duvet Designers, or John & Mary Parker, Miniature House Makers, or John & Mary Parker, Alternative Medicine Practitioners will not then be confused with each other.

Designing a letter heading is a fascinating way of spending an evening and alas, usually a bit of a waste of time. Apart from the fact that you might design something ostentatious (which scares off clients as they think you will be too dear), or wholly impractical (demanding typefaces that are unobtainable or designs that have to be hand drawn), the very unusual design could well prove highly expensive to produce. Printing firms and nowadays, photocopying services, can usually offer you a wide choice of typefaces and layouts that are in everyday use, and therefore, quite cheap. They will have someone on the staff who can design your headed notepaper too and they can show you a range of styles to choose from.

The right image

The sort of thing that you can influence because you know the sort of business you are in is layout and emphasis.

If, for example, you are setting up Beady Eye Detectives, you do want to emphasise the fact that you give an immediate response and guarantee confidentiality. So whilst you might want your company name and address on the left-hand side of the page, it could be very important to have the phone number with the words '24-hour answering service. Confidentiality guaranteed' on the right-hand side of the page.

If, on the other hand, you are John & Mary Parker, Miniature House Makers, and you are in the business of hand-making dolls' houses to match children's own homes, you might want a drawing to head your notepaper. To show that you are making houses in real-life style, you might choose a drawing of a modern house, which could be centred between the words 'Miniature House Makers' and 'Toys to Treasure' on the other.

If you can explain to the printers why you want the paper to present a particular image, you should find they are very helpful in showing you how it might be created at a reasonable cost. Choose standard sizes of notepaper and standard sizes for invoices. If money is very tight and you cannot afford to have both printed, you can set out

120

your invoices on paper of the same size as your letter heading. It may not be conventional practice, but it is accepted, and if it really worries you, take a pair of scissors and shorten the piece of notepaper used for an invoice!

Business cards are a good investment. Do not be tempted to have anything elaborate and over-sized. You want people to keep them in a card-case or wallet so they must fit conveniently.

Look for timesavers

What about envelopes? Here is a tip from long experience. Though you will want some conventional envelopes to match your letter heading for confidential letters, you can save a lot of envelope typing by using 'window' envelopes. It takes a bit of practice to get the address in the right place so that when you fold the letter or invoice, it shows clearly through the transparent window of the envelope, but it saves time in the long run, as do self-seal envelopes. You do not want to be constantly licking gum or even using a moistening sponge to stick down envelope flaps. Choose the self-seal kind but make sure they do self-seal – some are better than others.

If you are designing a leaflet to send out about your product or service, something that will fit conveniently into a standard size of envelope, or which can be folded up to fit a non-standard envelope is a bonus. Your small advertisement may say 'send s.a.e. for details'. Depend upon it, some people will send stamped addressed envelopes they appear to have kept from miniature Christmas cards for several years. On these occasions, you may have to use one of your own envelopes and your own stamps but, where possible, save money by letting interested clients make a contribution with their stamped addressed envelopes. It is not so much that pennies saved will make you a fortune (though many a successful business has grown from a careful watch on the pennies by a cost-paring owner). But using an s.a.e. save you time in buying stamps as well as using your own envelopes.

When you are ordering your stationery it is a good idea to take note of when the shop is open. You may want to dash in one afternoon to buy a large envelope for a batch of samples you have been asked to produce by a very promising client – only to discover that it is Thursday, and they shut at 1 p.m. on Thursday. Here is a piece of useful information for the Office Notebook.

Buy for your needs

Since stationery is the subject, as well as ordering printed note-paper, you will want copy paper (a thin type of paper for carbon copies) so you can keep evidence of what you have said; carbon paper and a slightly heavier kind of typing paper known as 'bank' for second pages. This other kind of paper may last you a very long time if you do not have to write reports or give lengthy quotations. But if your business is of the kind where your communications quite often run to two pages – quoting for building work, for instance – do not turn the page and use the back, use a second sheet of plain paper.

The thought of carbon copies will make you think about how you are going to store your correspondence. Stationery shops are a real temptation with their array of hanging files, coloured folders, box files, filing trays and the like. To begin with, buy some paper clips of different sizes and some bulldog clips for thicker batches of paper. As time goes on, you could well find you want to store certain kinds of record in coloured folders (*orders, suppliers, invoices, correspondence*) but you could still keep your folders in a stout cardboard box, buying a formal filing system when your business expands. You may want to store data on a computer. Which reminds me, do not forget a date stamp.

Essentials

To complete the basics, you could find that a diary, an address book and an Office Notebook are all you need in terms of quick reference guides, plus a notepad to keep by the phone. As time goes by, you may well want to make out a separate card for each client and devising a home-made card index or buying an inexpensive professional card index for them.

If you are in the kind of business where people often ring up about the progress of their order, and you need to refer to their order form, your job sheet and any correspondence, having one of those expanding cardboard files with pockets labelled *A, B, C* for each customer can be very useful to keep near the phone.

I am sure that it is possible to start some kinds of small business without a telephone of your own, but it must be extremely difficult. I have met journalists who have made use of a friend to answer their phone when they are doing freelance work whilst holding down a full-time job, and they do seem to manage to get messages through. However, I cannot help feeling that access to a phone is an essential, both from the point of view of customers who want to contact you, and your own need to chase up slow suppliers, pass on messages to people urgently and so on.

This must seem strange to you if you are working for a company which supplies telephones for both internal and external calls, and offers dozens of extensions. It is not until you start thinking how you might manage in business without the use of a phone that you value free access to one – and maybe make a better use of the phone facilities provided.

Speak after the tone . . .

If yours is a one-person business, a telephone that is combined with an answering machine for messages is a most valuable investment. Never mind that you have to keep your filing in cardboard boxes and you can only afford to order 1000 sheets of printed notepaper, being able to leave a pleasant message on your answering machine is a boon. (*See Chapter 3 Telephone skills*.) Do not buy in a hurry though; try several systems. You can get answering machines that allow you to hear the message being left, so that if you have put the answering machine on because you really do need some time without interruption, you can pick up the phone and speak to the person concerned if it proves to be urgent.

You can get answering machines with a remote control device that enables you to ring in from wherever you are, hear all your messages and then reset the machine. Brian Dee of Beady Eye Detectives could find this invaluable. He could get in touch with his potential client in Luton on his way home from Stevenage, and perhaps even arrange to call in, if the matter is very urgent.

Specialised telephone devices, like pagers, may be valuable for particular kinds of business. Couriers use them widely. I did meet one estate agent who had taken the plunge and gone into business for himself, and so had invested in the high cost of a car telephone. With thousands of pounds at stake, it was his most important business tool; enabling sellers and buyers to find him wherever he happened to be.

What did he say?

If you are using a telephone in a car or scrawling messages down in a telephone box, the best you can probably do is use a small notepad and capital letters (the more difficult your working conditions, the more important it is to write large and simply!). If you are taking messages using your own phone in the office, use a large pad with lines, and again, use block capitals for any names or addresses or vital parts of the message. Your normal characterful handwriting may be hard to read three days later, and impossible for anyone else to decipher if you go home with flu. And please, use dark, non-smudge pens!

With a new small business, think very carefully before you purchase anything that you can hire. It is very nice to have a typewriter and you may think that for the small use you would give one (quotations and invoices for your cake-icing business) any old second-hand typewriter will do. That is not necessarily so. If you have a good explanatory leaflet printed, with sizes and prices clearly set out, and if you can handwrite quotations on your letter heading, using a good quality carbon paper to keep a copy, that will probably be enough for you to manage with, especially if you have a secretarial service nearby where the odd business letter to suppliers can be typed.

Calculate the value

If your business expands, you could probably justify an electronic display typewriter (good for inexpert typists, as they can correct their mistakes), and much less strenuous to use than a manual. It would also be an attraction to any expert typist you may take on later.

A photocopier may be valuable in some kinds of business, but again, you can use the widely available photocopying services (which can include colour photocopying) until your business is firmly established. Some big companies are not too proud to do this and you also need a considerable turnover before you can invest in a fax machine, which transmits letters and diagrams down a telephone line.

This is perhaps a good place to say that second-hand office equipment can be very good value, but you need someone in the know to check it over. Desks with woodworm, typewriters with sticking numeral keys, and especially out-dated computers that you cannot have repaired are a real trap for the unwary.

Image again

What about office furniture? A lot depends on how long you are going to spend sitting at your desk and what storage space you need. Another factor to take into account is whether your clients will expect to be able to drop in on you. Image is important in the latter case. Your cardboard box files had better be kept in the bedroom, though you can often get away with quite a modest desk in the window of your living room provided you have a rather grand appointments book. Furniture warehouses offer cheap 'student desks' but check out how comfortable they are before you buy; what suits a teenager may not fit a 6'2" adult, and it is most unlikely to have been designed for making loose covers for

your upholstery business. You may well find that a work table is more suitable than a desk. An adjustable chair could be a very good investment; you can use it for cutting out, typing, icing or whatever, moving it up and down according to your needs. If your business involves a lot of sitting, **do not economise on furniture.** One sure-fire way of going bust is to strain your back so you cannot work.

Much of what I have said so far refers to someone working at home but you may be able to afford an office. There are good things and bad things about renting an office from which to operate. Certainly you are unlikely to be interrupted by a neighbour who wants to borrow a cup of sugar or a bag of muesli. On the other hand, burglars have a habit of spotting when people are out all day, so install an alarm system before you suddenly change your way of life after working at home.

Extras

In rented office property, you will usually have not only the cost of the rent, but the cost of the lease (which you will have to sign for a certain period) and extras like lighting, heating and cleaning to pay for. As a rule, office building managements have an agreement with a cleaning service and all tenants pay a contribution. If you happen to be reading this book as a set text on an office practice course, it can be very enlightening to check out the costs of renting office space in your town with one or two agents. You will never take your company's warm, carpeted premises with their drinks vending machine and clean loos for granted, ever again.

Partners, colleagues, part-timers

In other words, other pairs of hands. I think I have already emphasised the importance of having colleagues you can rely on, and in a small business, having someone you can turn to in an emergency, to keep your business ticking over until you get off your sick bed and stagger back to work.

If you are equipped with that entrepreneur's friend the answering machine, your helper can be a partner, husband or wife who takes over after the working day and at weekends and holds the fort with your guidance. They can refer recorded messages and queries to you for a decision on the right action to take. For example, if you offer some kind of specialised service, it may be preferable to show your good will by referring a client on to a competitor and retain your reputation for service. What would be best: simply to turn away that request to make a retirement cake, or to be able to say 'I'm sorry, I can't handle it at present, but there are other well-known cake-makers. You could try Bakeaway; they make cakes on customers' premises. Or there's Cause for Celebration; cake-making is one of their catering services.' I think you will find that, though you might lose that particular bit of business, people will remember your helpfulness and since you would lose the business anyway, you might as well try to benefit from the situation.

Apart from needing someone to stand in for you in emergency, sooner or later in most kinds of business, there is the need to train a newcomer. This is just as likely to be something that comes your way in the employment of a large company with a big office staff, as for the individual in a self-employment situation. However excellent the college course may have been and willing the learner, training in employment has challenges all of its own, both for newcomers and experienced office workers.

Learning the ropes

From working to general principles, the trainee has to adapt to a particular employer's style of working. This may come as a surprise. After all, they have been taught the right way to do things on their course. Accepting the necessity to 'cut corners' to work at a high speed, or to use a friendly style of conversation with potential customers when you may have been trained in a formal way can be hard for a newcomer. Bear this in mind when you are the person doing the training.

If it is your responsibility to choose and employ someone, begin by thinking about what the job entails and also what it offers. Employment is a two-way process. You might enjoy having someone lively and extrovert in your office to check purchase orders against deliveries and type standard letters, inserting the relevant names and addresses by hand, but they are not likely to stay long if that is the limit of their scope and they are ambitious. Better to take on the rather nervous youngster whose careers office describes as very willing to learn and good with routine work – or the mother returner who says she is nervous at the thought of learning how to combine work with domestic responsibilities and wants to ease herself back gradually.

Easing the load

Good staff are hard to find. It is a catchphrase, and like many a catchphrase, it has caught on because it is true. You may have to make a compromise when you are staffing your office and pick someone who does not have all the qualities or qualifications you had hoped for. So to go back to where we started and think about what the job entails. Is there anything that can be made easier? (using a calculator; using an in-expensive personal computer – many teenagers are trained to use these at school nowadays). Or would you do better to employ a 'superperson' part-time? Try out that married woman returner who has to leave at 3 p.m. every day and wants all school holidays off. Or can you get some of the work done by outworkers, directly or through an agency? If you are able to break down the work of the office into its component parts, you can then match the tasks to the talent available.

Which is where this book came in with Chapter 1 *What do you think you're doing?* If you are not sure you know, check your need for extra help against the kinds of work it explains. Meanwhile and

To sum up:

If you are equipping and staffing an office, it pays to:

- Think hard about the equipment you really need
- Match your business image to your product or service
- Look for time and money-savers
- Compare the costs of hiring and buying
- Check the pros and cons of renting an office
- Concentrate on essential skills when choosing staff
- Pay for what you need – wait for what you want!

My thanks to the many office staff whose advice and ideas contributed to this book, particularly those with whom I worked.